Quest

Teacher's Edition

1

 **Listening and Speaking**

Student Book Authors
Laurie Blass
Pamela Hartmann

Teacher's Edition Writer
Kristin Sherman

 **McGraw-Hill**

Quest 1 Listening and Speaking Teacher's Edition

Published by McGraw-Hill ESL/ELT, a business unit of The McGraw-Hill Companies, Inc. 1221 Avenue of the Americas, New York, NY 10020.

ISBN13: 978-0-07-326709-8
ISBN10: 0-07-326709-0
 2 3 4 5 6 7 8 9 QPD 12 11 10 09 08 07 06

Editorial director: Erik Gundersen
Series editor: Linda O'Roke
Development editor: Dylan Bryan-Dolman
Production manager: Juanita Thompson
Production coordinator: James D. Gwyn
Cover designer: David Averbach, Anthology
Interior designer: Karolyn Wehner

www.esl-elt.mcgraw-hill.com

The *McGraw-Hill* Companies

TABLE OF CONTENTS

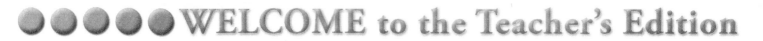

WELCOME to the Teacher's Edition

The *Quest* Teacher's Edition provides support and flexibility to teachers using the *Quest* Student Book. Each chapter of the Teacher's Edition begins with a chapter overview which includes a brief summary of the Student Book chapter, a list of the vocabulary words found in the chapter, a list of the reading, critical thinking, and writing strategies highlighted throughout the chapter, as well as a list of the mechanics presented and practiced in that chapter. In addition, the Teacher's Edition provides step-by-step teaching procedures; notes on culture, grammar, vocabulary, and pronunciation; expansion activities; photocopiable masters of select expansion activities; Internet research ideas; answer keys; and end-of-chapter tests.

Procedures

○ Experienced teachers can use the step-by-step procedural notes as a quick guide and refresher before class, while newer or substitute teachers can use the notes as a more extensive guide in the classroom. These notes also help teachers provide context for the activities and assess comprehension of the material covered.

Answer Keys

○ Answer keys are provided for all activities that have definite answers. In cases where multiple answers could be correct, possible answers are included. Answer keys are also provided for the Vocabulary Workshop after each unit.

Notes

○ Where appropriate, culture, grammar, academic, and pronunciation notes provide background information, answers to questions students might raise, or points teachers might want to review or introduce. For example, in *Quest 1 Listening and Speaking* Chapter 2, a reading refers to Ralph Lauren, so a cultural note provides some background information on this designer. These notes are provided at the logical point of use, but teachers can decide if and when to use the information in class.

TOEFL® iBT Tips

○ In each chapter, six tips for the TOEFL iBT are given with corresponding notes on how strategies and activities from the student book chapter can help students practice and prepare for the exam. Examples of TOEFL iBT question formats are also given in these tips.

Expansion Activities

○ At least 10 optional expansion activities are included in each chapter. These activities offer teachers creative ideas for reinforcing the chapter content while appealing to different learning styles. Activities include games, conversation practice, working with manipulatives such as sentence strips, projects, and presentations. These expansion activities often allow students to practice all four language skills, not just the two skills that the student book focuses on.

Photocopiable Masters

○ Up to three master worksheets that teachers can photocopy are included after each chapter. These worksheets are optional and are described in expansion activities located within the chapter. One chapter worksheet is often additional editing practice, while the others might be a graphic organizer or a set of sentence strips.

End-of-Chapter Tests

○ The end-of-chapter tests assess students on reading comprehension, one or more of the reading or critical thinking strategies highlighted in the chapter, vocabulary, mechanics, and editing. Item types include multiple choice, fill-in-the-blank, and true/false, for a total of 35 items per test. Answer keys are provided.

Scope and Sequence

Chapter	Listening Strategies	Speaking Strategies
UNIT 1 BUSINESS		
Chapter 1: Career Planning • Social Language: Advice about Starting College • Broadcast English: Radio Program about College Today and College 50 Years Ago, and Advice for New Students • Academic English: Lecture by a Career Counselor to English-Language Students	• Understanding the Medial *T* • Taking Notes: Using a Graphic Organizer • Listening for Details • Taking Notes: Using an Outline • Understanding New Words • Organizing Your Notes: Paying Attention to Signposts	• Asking and Answering Comparison Questions • Giving Advice • Planning Ahead • Asking for Clarification
Chapter 2: The Global Economy • Social Language: Conversation about Products in the Global Economy • Broadcast English: Radio Program about Successful Textile Companies in China • Academic English: Lecture about a U.S. Company	• Listening for Supporting Information • Identifying a Causal Chain • Listening for an Anecdote • Asking Questions	• Outlining • Making Eye Contact
UNIT 2 BIOLOGY		
Chapter 3: Animal Behavior • Social Language: Conversation about Animals' Emotions and Intelligence • Broadcast English: Radio Program about Research on Language Learning in Animals • Academic English: Lecture about Humans and Animals	• Understanding Emotion from Tone of Voice • Previewing: Thinking Before Listening • Knowing When to Take Notes • Including Details in Your Notes	• Using Nonverbal Communication • Expressions of Disbelief and Skepticism

The Mechanics of Listening and Speaking	Critical Thinking Strategies	Test-Taking Strategies
UNIT 1 BUSINESS		
• Asking for Directions • Understanding Interjections • /θ/ vs. /s/ • Expressions for Giving Directions	• Interpreting Information on Tables • Recognizing Literal and Figurative Meanings	• Guessing the Meaning from Context
• *Wh-* Questions • Greeting People You Know • Responding to Greetings: General and Specific • Returning Greetings • Reduced Forms of Words • Expressions with *Look, Seem,* and *Sound* + Adjective	• Previewing: Brainstorming • Making Connections	• Making Predictions
UNIT 2 BIOLOGY		
• Changing Statements into Questions • Agreeing with Negative Questions • Disagreeing with Negative Questions • Reduced Forms of Words • Expressions of Disbelief and Skepticism	• Making Inferences • Understanding a Speaker's Point of View	• Listening for Stressed Words

Chapter	Listening Strategies	Speaking Strategies
Chapter 4: Nutrition • Social Language: Conversation about Food and Nutrition • Broadcast English: Radio Program about the Diet of the People in the Mediterranean Region • Academic English: Lecture about Nutrition	• Listening for Numerical Information • Guessing the Meaning from Context: *Such As* • Previewing: Asking Questions Before You Listen • Getting the Main Ideas from the Introduction • Listening for Categories and Definitions	• Taking Turns • Giving More Information: Reasons or Examples
UNIT 3 U.S. HISTORY		
Chapter 5: The Days of Slavery • Social Language: Conversation Between a Student and a Professor about an Assignment • Broadcast English: Radio Program about the Underground Railroad • Academic English: Lecture about the Underground Railroad	• Being Prepared for an Important Explanation • Listening for Examples in Groups • Listening for Dates	• Working Cooperatively • Giving and Getting Feedback
Chapter 6: U.S. History Through Film • Social Language: Conversation about a Movie • Broadcast English: Radio Program about Westerns • Academic English: Lecture about U.S. History as Seen Through Film	• Review: Taking Lecture Notes	• Talking about Symbols • Taking a Survey

The Mechanics of Listening and Speaking	Critical Thinking Strategies	Test-Taking Strategies
• Asking for More Information: Reasons • Asking for More Information: Examples • Giving More Information: Reasons or Examples • Reduced Forms of Words: Questions with *Do* and *Did* • Noun Phrases for Types of Food	• Comparing Sources of Information	• Listening for Reasons

UNIT 3 U.S. HISTORY

• Introducing Yourself to Someone Who Doesn't Remember You • Responding to an Introduction • Identifying Yourself on the Phone • /I/ vs. /i/ • Verb Phrases for Meeting People	• Using a Timeline	• Previewing: Brainstorming Possible Vocabulary
• Verbs Ending in *-ed* • Giving an Opinion • Agreeing and Disagreeing • Showing Disagreement with Intonation	• Synthesizing	• Review: Taking Lecture Notes

Introduction

GETTING STARTED

In this chapter, students will listen to a two-part lecture about the basics of higher education in the United States and Canada and will practice note-taking. Students will practice listening and speaking strategies, including how to understand and use correct intonation in tag questions. Finally, students will listen to a call-in radio program.

VOCABULARY

campus	freshman	make small talk	sophomore
college	graduate school	master's degree	synonym
community college	junior	phrase	tag question
definition	lecture	reply	undergraduate
degree	major	senior	university
doctor of philosophy			

LISTENING STRATEGIES

Taking Lecture Notes
Finding Practice Opportunities
Understanding the Intonation of Tag Questions
Listening for the Main Idea
Understanding Fast or Difficult English

SPEAKING STRATEGIES

Finding Practice Opportunities
Making Small Talk
Using Tag Questions

MECHANICS OF LISTENING AND SPEAKING

Words in Phrases: Talking about Your Major

Getting Started Opener, page 1

❍ Put students in pairs to discuss the questions.
❍ Call on students to share their ideas with the class.

INTRODUCTION TO ACADEMIC LIFE, PAGES 2–7

❍ Go over the information at the top of page 2.
❍ Put students in pairs or small groups to brainstorm things they can expect and things they need to do to go to school in the United States or Canada.
❍ Elicit ideas from the class and write them on the board.

🎧 A. Listening to a Lecture: Section 1

❍ Go over the directions.
❍ Direct students' attention to the reading.
❍ Have students read along as you play the audio program.
❍ Have students close their books as they listen for a second time.

LISTENING STRATEGY: Taking Lecture Notes

❍ Go over the information in the box.
❍ Ask comprehension questions: *What is a lecture? Is the information in lectures the same as the information in the textbook? What are some things you should do when you take notes? How can you tell that a professor is giving a definition? What is a synonym?*

EXPANSION ACTIVITY: Beanbag Toss

❍ Give students two minutes to review the information in the reading.
❍ After two minutes, ask students to close their books.
❍ Explain that you will call on a student and say a word or phrase from the reading (e.g., *freshman year*) as you toss a beanbag or ball. The student should catch the beanbag, give the correct definition (e.g., *first year in college*) of the word, and toss the beanbag back.
❍ Call on a student, toss the beanbag and say a word. Elicit the definition.
❍ Continue the activity until all the words have been defined or all the students have had a chance to participate.

B. Taking Lecture Notes

❍ Go over the directions.
❍ Direct students' attention to the lecture outline on page 4. Ask questions about the notes: *What are the three main topics? How many years are undergraduate students usually in school? What is the term for students in graduate school?*
❍ Put students in pairs to compare the lecture and the notes.
❍ Call on students to share their ideas with the class.

ANSWER KEY

Answers will vary.

EXPANSION ACTIVITY: Class Outline

❍ Photocopy the worksheet *Class Outline* on page BLM 1. Cut between each line, making strips of paper.
❍ Give students a minute to review the outline on page 4, and then instruct them to close their books.
❍ Give each student a strip of paper. Have students stand and move around the room to reconstruct the outline of the lecture from memory.
❍ Have students stand in a line to represent the outline (i.e., the first student should have the slip *Undergraduate Students*, and the last student should have *U.S.: I'm in college*).
❍ Have students read their slips aloud. Encourage students to reposition themselves if necessary.

🎧 C. Listening to a Lecture: Section 2

❍ Go over the directions.
❍ Have students take notes on the outline as you play the audio program.
❍ Play the audio program again if necessary.
❍ Have students compare their notes in pairs.
❍ Go over the answers with the class. Reconstruct the outline on the board if necessary.

AUDIO SCRIPT

Lecturer: For your freshman and sophomore years in the United States (but not in Canada), you'll take mostly general education requirements. General education requirements are basic classes in many different subjects—an introduction to biology, history, art, psychology, anthropology, English, and so on. All students must take the general education requirements. There's no escape! However, there is also space for you to take electives. Electives are classes that you *choose* to take. It's a good idea—and this is important—to choose electives in a number of different subjects that interest you. This is the time to explore, to discover new things.

Soon you'll need to decide on a major. Your major is your main area, your main field of study. In your first two years—your freshman and sophomore years—you'll take *some* classes in your major but not many. In your third and fourth years—your junior and senior years—almost all of your classes will be in your major. When you graduate, you will have a degree in your major. For example, you might have a B.A. in history or a B.S. in chemistry.

ANSWER KEY

College in the United States and Canada
Section 2
   I. General Education Requirements (U.S. only)
      A. Definition: <u>basic classes in many different subjects</u>
      B. Examples: <u>biology, history, art, psychology, anthropology, English</u>
   II. Electives
      A. Definition: <u>classes you choose to take</u>
      B. Good idea to: <u>choose electives in a number of different subjects that interest you</u>
   III. Major
      A. Definition: <u>main area, main field of study</u>
      B. Freshman and sophomore years: <u>take some classes in major, not many</u>
      C. Junior and senior years: <u>almost all of your classes will be in your major</u>

WORDS IN PHRASES: Talking about Your Major
○ Go over the information in the box.
○ Ask comprehension questions: *What is a phrase? What is an example of a phrase?*

D. Words in Phrases
○ Go over the directions. Ask a student to read the role of Student A in the example, while you read the role of Student B.
○ Direct students' attention to the chart. Copy the chart headings on the board.
○ Model the activity. Call on a student and ask the questions that Student A asks in the example. Write the student's answers on the board.
○ Have students walk around the room and ask classmates about their majors, then write the answers on the chart.
○ Call on students to tell the class about a classmate.

ANSWER KEY
Answers will vary.

EXPANSION ACTIVITY: Write Sentences
○ Have students write sentences about three of their classmates, using the expressions in the box.
○ Put students in pairs to read their sentences.

INTRODUCTION TO LISTENING AND SPEAKING, PAGES 8–15
○ Go over the information at the beginning of this section.
○ Ask comprehension questions: *What types of English will you hear in this book? What situations will you practice speaking in?*

EXPANSION ACTIVITY: What Makes You Uncomfortable?
○ Point out that students often feel uncomfortable or even a little afraid when they are learning a new language.

○ Have students write down their feelings about listening and speaking in the different types of English and situations listed on page 8.
○ Put students in pairs to share their ideas.

LISTENING STRATEGY: Finding Practice Opportunities

○ Go over the information in the box.
○ Ask comprehension questions: *What can you do to improve your listening ability in English? Which practice opportunity do you think you would like best?*

SPEAKING STRATEGY: Finding Practice Opportunities

○ Go over the information in the box.
○ Ask comprehension questions: *Which idea seems the easiest to you? Which would be the most difficult?*

A. Finding Practice Opportunities

○ Go over the directions.
○ Have students work in small groups to list places where they can practice English.
○ Call on students from each group to share at least one idea with the class.

EXPANSION ACTIVITY: Make a Commitment

○ Ask students to choose one or more practice opportunities to try.
○ Have students schedule time for their practice opportunities in their planners or agenda.
○ Call on students to share their ideas with the class.

SPEAKING STRATEGY: Making Small Talk

○ Go over the information in the box.
○ Ask comprehension questions: *What is small talk? When do people make small talk? What is a tag question? What types of things do people talk about when they make small talk?*

B. Making Small Talk

○ Go over the directions and the questions.
○ Have students discuss the questions in small groups.
○ Call on students to share their ideas with the class.

ANSWER KEY
Answers will vary.

SPEAKING STRATEGY: Using Tag Questions

○ Go over the information in the box.
○ Ask comprehension questions: *What is an example of a tag? If the statement is* The test was hard, *what is the tag? Why do we use tag questions?*

C. Using Tag Questions

○ Go over the directions.
○ Have students write a tag question to complete each sentence and then compare answers with a partner.
○ Go over the answers with the class.

ANSWER KEY
1. aren't they?; 2. doesn't it?; 3. wasn't it?; 4. does it?; 5. aren't they?; 6. isn't it?; 7. was it?; 8. wasn't it?; 9. did we?; 10. is it?

EXPANSION ACTIVITY: Tag Question Relay

○ Explain the activity. Tell the class that each student will say a statement in turn. The next person must add the appropriate tag for that statement.
○ Make a statement (*It's a beautiful day*). Call on a student and elicit the correct tag (*isn't it?*). Encourage that student to make a statement. Ask the student next to him or her to supply the correct tag.
○ Continue until everyone has had a chance to participate.

LISTENING STRATEGY: Understanding the Intonation of Tag Questions

○ Go over the information in the box and play the audio program.
○ Ask comprehension questions: *What kind of intonation do we use when we really need information?* (Your voice goes up.) *What intonation do we use when we already know the answer?* (Your voice goes down.)

D. Understanding the Intonation of Tag Questions

- ○ Go over the directions.
- ○ Have students circle *Yes* or *No* as you play the audio program.
- ○ Put students in pairs to compare answers.
- ○ Go over the answers with the class.
- ○ Play the audio program a second time and have students repeat in the pauses between the sentences.

Audio Script

1. They're busy, aren't they? *[Falling Intonation]*
2. This bus goes to Brand Street, doesn't it? *[Rising Intonation]*
3. It was a great movie, wasn't it? *[Falling Intonation]*
4. This bus doesn't go to Riverside, does it? *[Falling Intonation]*
5. The biology books are over there, aren't they? *[Rising Intonation]*
6. The food at this party is fabulous, isn't it? *[Falling Intonation]*
7. The test wasn't very hard, was it? *[Falling Intonation]*
8. The homework was interesting, wasn't it? *[Falling Intonation]*
9. We didn't have to do Chapter 5, did we? *[Rising Intonation]*
10. The history department isn't offering History 207 this term, is it? *[Falling Intonation]*

ANSWER KEY

1. No; 2. Yes; 3. No; 4. No; 5. Yes; 6. No; 7. No; 8. No; 9. Yes; 10. No

E. Understanding the Intonation of Tag Questions

- ○ Go over the directions.
- ○ Have students circle *Real question* or *Small talk* as you play the audio program.
- ○ Play the audio program again if necessary.
- ○ Put students in pairs to compare answers.
- ○ Go over the answers with the class.

Audio Script

1. **A:** Boy, it's hot today, isn't it? *[Falling Intonation]*
   B: Yeah, it really is.
2. **A:** This bus doesn't run on time too often, does it? *[Rising Intonation]*
   B: No, it doesn't.
3. **A:** They're pretty slow at fixing the air conditioning around here, aren't they? *[Falling Intonation]*
   B: They sure are.
4. **A:** They look nice, don't they? *[Falling Intonation]*
   B: Yeah, they do.
5. **A:** You haven't ever taken Business 251, have you? *[Rising Intonation]*
   B: No, I haven't.

ANSWER KEY

1. Small Talk; 2. Real Question; 3. Small Talk; 4. Small Talk; 5. Real Question

F. Using Tag Questions in Conversations

- ○ Go over the directions.
- ○ Read the situations in each example and have two students read each conversation with the appropriate intonation. Make sure Student A uses rising intonation in the first example and falling intonation in the second example.
- ○ Put students in pairs to take turns asking and responding to tag questions. Remind students to take turns playing the role of Student A.
- ○ Walk around the room to monitor the activity and provide help as needed.

LISTENING STRATEGY: Listening for the Main Idea

- ○ Go over the information in the box.
- ○ Ask comprehension questions: *What should you really try to listen for? What are some ways you can notice the main idea? What is* not *a main idea?*

G. Listening for the Main Idea

- ○ Go over the directions and the possible main ideas.
- ○ Tell students to fill in the bubble of the main idea as you play the audio program. Play the audio program as many times as necessary.

Audio Script

Penkava: O.K., we go to Daniel in Hollywood, Florida. Hi there, Daniel.
Daniel: How are you?
Penkava: O.K. How are you?
Daniel: Good. I'm calling because I think I have a somewhat interesting, uh, vantage point. I mean, my one piece of advice, and it's hard for some, 'cause I don't know how much I'd be listening to this if I was sort of entering college and just real excited to have my parents, as someone put it, drop off the radar screen. But, um, but really just study what you like and, uh, things will fall into place.
Penkava: Well, Daniel, thanks for your call and your advice.

ANSWER KEY
C

LISTENING STRATEGY: Understanding Fast or Difficult English

○ Go over the information in the box.
○ Ask comprehension questions: *What does* shy *mean? Why should you try not to be shy? How can you ask someone to repeat something you didn't understand? How can you practice listening to fast or difficult English?*

H. Understanding Fast or Difficult English

○ Go over the directions.
○ Ask students to read the statements.
○ Have students fill in T for *True* or F for *False* as you play the audio program.
○ Repeat more than once if necessary.
○ Go over the answers with the class.

Audio Script

Levine: By the way, I think that's a great piece of advice. I remember meeting a young woman, and I asked her what she was majoring in, and she said business, and I said, "Hey, that's great. How do you like it?" She said, "I absolutely hate it!" And I asked her, "What would you rather be majoring in?" And she said

"Dance," and I said, "Why don't you major in dance?" And her answer was, "Money is nice, poor is not nice, and I want nice." The sad part about this young woman was she gave up all of her dreams. Too many people give up their dreams too early.

ANSWER KEY
1. True; 2. True; 3. False; 4. True; 5. False; 6. True; 7. True

I. Discussion

○ Go over the directions and the questions.
○ Have students discuss the questions in small groups.
○ Call on students to share their ideas with the class.

ANSWER KEY
Answers will vary.

UNIT 1  BUSINESS

Unit Opener, page 17

○ Direct students' attention to the photo and the unit and chapter titles on page 17.
○ Brainstorm ideas about what the unit will include and write students' ideas on the board.

CHAPTER 1 CAREER PLANNING

In Part 1, students will look at tables of statistics related to educational levels, salaries, and trends in occupations. In Part 2, students will listen to advice for people just starting college. In Part 4, students will listen to a radio broadcast in which a university president, a writer, and a caller to the program talk about college today. In Part 5, students will listen to a lecture about five keys to academic success for ESL students. Finally, students will explore the websites of two colleges or universities to find out interesting features of the schools.

VOCABULARY

advantage	data	income	percent	signpost
advice	disadvantage	inference	physician	silly
aide	drop out	informal outline	process	skills
appeal to	experiment	joy	quarter	statistic
apply yourself	figurative	key	roughly	textile
assistant	formal outline	kiss your feet	seek out	tutor
career	get sucked in	literal	self-assessment	values
contrast	higher education	majority	set	workshop

LISTENING STRATEGIES

Understanding the Medial *T*
Taking Notes: Using a Graphic Organizer
Listening for Details
Taking Lecture Notes: Using an Outline
Understanding New Words
Organizing Your Notes: Paying Attention to Signposts

CRITICAL THINKING STRATEGIES

Thinking Ahead (Part 1)
Interpreting Information on Tables (Part 1)
Synthesizing (Part 3)
Recognizing Literal and Figurative Meanings (Part 4)
Note: Strategies in bold are highlighted in the Student Book.

MECHANICS OF LISTENING AND SPEAKING

Language Function: Asking for Directions
Intonation: Understanding Interjections
Pronunciation: /θ/ vs. /s/
Words in Phrases: Expressions for Giving Directions

SPEAKING STRATEGIES

Asking and Answering Comparison Questions
Giving Advice
Planning Ahead
Asking for Clarification

TEST-TAKING STRATEGY

Guessing the Meaning from Context

CHAPTER 1 Career Planning

Chapter 1 Opener, page 19

❍ Direct students' attention to the photo and chapter title. Go over the directions and questions.
❍ Put students in pairs to discuss the questions.
❍ Call on students to share their ideas with the class.

PART 1 INTRODUCTION
EDUCATION AND CAREER SUCCESS, PAGES 20–24

CRITICAL THINKING STRATEGY: Thinking Ahead

❍ Thinking ahead is an important critical thinking skill.
❍ It allows students to anticipate the content of what they will hear, which in turn promotes comprehension.

A. Thinking Ahead

❍ Go over the directions and the questions.
❍ Put students in pairs to answer the questions.
❍ Call on students to share their ideas with the class.

ANSWER KEY
Answers will vary.

EXPANSION ACTIVITY: Category Sort

❍ Tell students that you are going to ask some questions. They will respond by moving around the room to stand with classmates who have the same or similar answers. Point out that they should ask classmates the question in order to sort themselves by the answers they give. Encourage students to form distinct groups according to answer.
❍ Ask the question: *What is your major?* or *What do you plan to major in?* Remind students to sort themselves by answer. When students have formed groups, call on someone from each group to tell the class their

answer to the question (for example, *business*).
❍ Ask several more questions. Create your own or use the ones below.
What is most important to you in a job?
What kind of salary do you want/expect?
What can you do in college that will help you the most in your career?

B. Reading Tables

❍ Direct students' attention to the tables on pages 21–22 and ask comprehension questions: *What are these? What kind of information can you find in them?*
❍ Go over the directions and the questions.
❍ Have students read the tables and answer the questions.

ANSWER KEY
The more education a person has, the higher their income. Jobs from Table B (mostly in health care and computers) will be easy to find. Jobs from Table C will be hard to find.

Culture Notes

❍ You may want to present or review different levels of education in the United States. Most public school systems offer elementary school (kindergarten through 5th grade, or until about age 10), middle school (6th through 8th grades, or until about age 13), and high school or secondary school (9th through 12th grades, or until about age 18).
❍ Sometimes students can go to a vocational school at the secondary level, or after receiving a high school diploma. Vocational schools offer education and training that prepares students for job fields.
❍ Community colleges, sometimes called junior colleges, offer two-year degrees, either in general education which will transfer to a four-year university, or specific careers such as dental hygiene.

EXPANSION ACTIVITY: Tables at a Glance
○ Direct students to the Department of Labor website: http://www.bls.gov/eag/home.htm
○ Have students choose a state from the pull-down menu on the right (*Other Available At a Glance Tables*).
○ Ask students to note trends over time for that state (e.g., unemployment rate, manufacturing, leisure and hospitality, construction).
○ Call on students to share what they learned with the class.

C. Comprehension Check
○ Go over the directions and the questions.
○ Have students discuss the questions in small groups.
○ Go over the answers with the class.

ANSWER KEY
1. Doctorate; 2. some high school; 3. medical assistants; 4. telephone operators

CRITICAL THINKING STRATEGY: Interpreting Information on Tables
○ Go over the information in the box.
○ Ask comprehension questions: *What do tables give? What are statistics? What are some suggestions that can help you interpret these tables?*

D. Interpreting Information on Tables
○ Go over the directions and the questions.
○ Have students discuss the questions in small groups.
○ Call on students to share their ideas with the class.

ANSWER KEY
Answers will vary.
1. more education; 2. healthcare and computers; 3. textile/sewing; 4. They don't require a lot of education; 5. The elderly usually need the most care, and they are the group that is growing the fastest; 6. Many of the occupations can be done more cheaply overseas; 7. Other countries might be gaining in the areas where the U.S. is losing jobs.

E. Ranking Values
○ Go over the directions. Make sure students understand what *values* are.
○ Have students rank the list in order from 1 to 12.

ANSWER KEY
Answers will vary.

SPEAKING STRATEGY: Asking and Answering Comparison Questions
○ Go over the information in the box and the examples.
○ Model the activity. Make a statement about your own values, then ask a student about his or her values: *What's most important to you?*

TOEFL® iBT Tip

TOEFL iBT Tip 1: The independent speaking tasks on the TOEFL iBT require examinees to express and justify their preferences and dislikes.

○ Show students how the speaking strategy *Asking and Answering Comparison Questions* will help them to differentiate between their preferences and dislikes by using the correct comparative forms.

○ Point out that the rules for comparative forms in English have to be learned, and that reviewing the forms will help them prepare for this type of question on the test.

F. Asking and Answering Comparison Questions
○ Put students in pairs to talk about their value rankings.
○ Call on students to share their ideas with the class.

G. Journal Writing
○ Go over the directions.
○ Explain that this is a freewriting activity and does not have to be perfect. Point out that journal writing can be a warm-up to more structured writing.
○ Set a time limit of five minutes.
○ Put students in pairs to read or talk about their writing.

PART ② SOCIAL LANGUAGE
COLLEGE FOR BEGINNERS, PAGES 24–30

Before Listening

SPEAKING STRATEGY: Giving Advice
- Go over the information in the box.
- Ask comprehension questions: *When do you give advice? What is advice? What is an example of affirmative advice? What is an example of negative advice?*

Grammar Notes
- You may want to review the grammar rules students should follow with each structure presented in the strategy box.
- Commands are formed using the simple form of the main verb and no stated subject (implied subject is *you*). The negative command begins with *don't.*
- When using modals (e.g., *should*), the modal is followed by the simple form of the main verb.
- *Be sure to* is actually a phrase in the command form. It is followed by the simple form because the *to* is part of the infinitive. The negative is formed by *be sure* followed by *not + to + simple form of main verb*. The negative comes before the infinitive (*be sure + not + infinitive*).

A. Giving Advice
- Go over the directions.
- Have students complete the chart with affirmative and negative advice. Remind students to use different structures for giving advice.

B. Comparing Ideas
- Go over the directions.
- Have students share their charts in small groups.
- Ask representatives from each group to tell the class about advice that all or most of them included.

EXPANSION ACTIVITY: Venn Diagram
- Explain that Venn diagrams are graphic organizers that students can use to compare and contrast two things.
- Photocopy and distribute the worksheet *Comparing Advice* on page BLM 2.
- Draw a Venn diagram on the board like the one on BLM 2.
- Model the activity. Call on two students and ask them to read you some of the advice they wrote on their charts in Activity A. Write the advice in the correct place on the diagram. Write advice that both students wrote in the overlapping section in the middle, and put advice that only one student wrote in one of the two outside sections.
- Put students in pairs to compare advice and complete the Venn diagrams.
- Call on students to share with the class similarities and differences they had with their partners.

C. Thinking Ahead
- Go over the directions.
- Have students work in pairs to predict six pieces of advice that they will hear on the video.
- Call on students to share ideas with the class.

Listening
🎦 🎧 A. Listening for the Main Idea
- Go over the directions and the question.
- Play the video or audio program.
- Ask students: *What advice do most speakers give?*

Audio Script
Evan: Hi, how are you doing?
Speaker 1: Hi, I'm well, thanks.
Evan: What's your name?
Speaker 1: Kay.
Evan: Well, I'm doing an interview for Campus TV. Would you mind if I asked you a couple of questions?
Speaker 1: No, that's fine, go ahead.
Evan: What advice, if anything, would you give to students starting in college?
Speaker 1: Um, I would advise them not to be afraid to ask questions that they think are silly or stupid because chances are other people have the same questions, and if you don't ask, you never get the answers.

Speaker 2: I think the most important thing is to, um, manage your time well, to, um, apply yourself after classes, to put in an equal effort, like, review classes as much as—if the class is an hour and a half, you study for at least an hour and a half just to review things.

Speaker 3: So, I guess the advice that I would take from somebody would be to choose their school wisely and to realize that that's going to be your future right there.

Speaker 4: Take classes in areas that you would never think you would be interested in—um, learning about, um—totally just using it as a time to open yourself up to other things and other ideas.

Evan: What advice can you give to students just beginning college?

Speaker 5: Meet new people. And, ah, really learn new things, not just from books but from, you know, the people and—

Evan: Be open-minded?

Speaker 5: Yes, be more open-minded—that's what I meant to say. Yeah, that's it.

Speaker 6: I would say, you know, take full advantage of the resources that are available to you. Meet as many different people as possible from as many different backgrounds.

Speaker 7: Oh, just beginning college, probably be academically prepared and, you know, don't get sucked in by social pressures.

Evan: Don't party too much.

Speaker 7: That's right.

Speaker 8: I think that college students should remember that they're here to learn, not just to party.

Speaker 9: Don't worry about what major you're going to have 'cause invariably it changes.

Speaker 10: Relax. Stop worrying so much about my career, my future, and enjoy what you're learning.

Speaker 11: Have fun.

Evan: Have fun.

Speaker 11: Don't take it all that seriously.

ANSWER KEY

To do something else (ask questions, choose their school wisely, be open to new things, meet new people, relax)

🎧 B. Listening for Details

○ Go over the directions.
○ Have students complete the chart as you play the video or audio program a second time.
○ Put students in pairs to compare answers.
○ Go over the answers with the class.

ANSWER KEY

Some answers may vary.

Speaker	Work/ Study Hard	Enjoy Yourself/ Have Fun	Something Else
1			✔
2	✔		
3			✔
4			✔
5			✔
6			✔
7	✔		
8	✔		
9			✔
10		✔	
11		✔	

EXPANSION ACTIVITY: Who is Like You?

○ Ask students which of the people in the video is most like them and who is most unlike them.
○ Put students in pairs to share their ideas.
○ Call on students to share their ideas with the class.

TEST-TAKING STRATEGY: Guessing the Meaning from Context

○ Go over the information in the box.
○ Ask questions: *Should you use a dictionary when you listen to a conversation? What should you do instead? What is* context?

TOEFL® iBT Tip

TOEFL iBT Tip 2: On the TOEFL iBT, there will be a wide range of vocabulary words in context that provide important clues to the topic of the conversation or lecture.

○ Point out that the test-taking strategy *Guessing the Meaning from Context* will help students identify words or terms that are new or unfamiliar. Understanding the words that are near or *around* the new word is useful for both the academic lectures and campus-based conversations.

○ Remind students that focusing on words that they *do* understand will help them to get the general meaning of an item on the test, especially when time limits how quickly they must comprehend a conversation or lecture in order to respond to a question.

C. Guessing the Meaning from Context

○ Go over the directions.
○ Have students write their guesses on the lines as you play the video or audio program.
○ Go over the answers with the class.

Audio Script

1. **Speaker 1:** Um, I would advise them not to be afraid to ask questions that they think are silly or stupid because chances are other people have the same questions, and if you don't ask, you never get the answers.
2. **Speaker 2:** I think the most important thing is to, um, manage your time well, to, um, apply yourself after classes, to put in an equal effort like, review classes as much as—if the class is an hour and a half, you study for at least an hour and a half just to review things.
3. **Speaker 7:** Oh, just beginning college, probably be academically prepared and, you know, don't get sucked in by social pressures.
   Evan: Don't party too much.
   Speaker 7: That's right.

ANSWER KEY
1. stupid; 2. to put in an equal effort; 3. don't party too much

Academic Note
○ Point out to students that context provides clues to the meaning of a word in that particular situation and may not always apply to other contexts.

D. Listening for Specific Ideas

○ Go over the directions.
○ Instruct students to write their answers on the lines as you play the video or audio program.
○ Have students check their answers in pairs.
○ Go over the answers with the class.

Audio Script

1. **Speaker 1:** Um, I would advise them not to be afraid to ask questions that they think are silly or stupid because chances are other people have the same questions, and if you don't ask, you never get the answers.
2. **Speaker 2:** I think the most important thing is to, um, manage your time well, to um, apply yourself after classes, to put in an equal effort like, review classes as much as—if the class is an hour and a half, you study for at least an hour and a half just to review things.
3. **Speaker 5:** Meet new people. And ah—
   Evan: Be open-minded?
   Speaker 5: Yes, be more open-minded—that's what I meant to say. Yeah, that's it.
4. **Speaker 9:** Don't worry about what major you're going to have 'cause invariably it changes.

ANSWER KEY

1. because if you don't ask, you never get the answers
2. at least an equal amount of time as the class
3. meet new people
4. about a major because it will change

Culture Note

○ Students in the United States often change their majors at some point during college. This is considered normal and does not harm the students' reputations.

After Listening

A. Discussion

○ Go over the directions and the questions.
○ Put students in small groups to discuss the questions.
○ Call on students to share their ideas with the class.

SPEAKING STRATEGY: Planning Ahead

○ Go over the information in the box.
○ Ask questions: *Why should you plan ahead? What steps should you follow?*

B. Planning Ahead

○ Go over the directions and the answers.
○ Direct students' attention to the first answer and ask *How do you know what question was asked?*
○ Make clear that students should write questions that can be answered by the words in red.
○ Have students write questions.
○ Go over the questions with the class.
○ Put students in pairs to practice asking and answering the questions.

ANSWER KEY

Answers will vary.
1. How are you?
2. What is his name?
3. When is the library open?
4. What do we have to read?
5. When does the class meet?
6. Was the test hard?

7. What does *T.A.* mean?
8. Is it far?
9. Where is the counseling center?
10. How do you get to the copy center?

C. Asking the Right Questions

○ Go over the directions and situations.
○ Read the first situation and elicit questions.
○ Have students write questions to ask in each situation and then compare questions with a partner.
○ Call on students to read their questions to the class.

ANSWER KEY

Answers will vary.
1. Could you repeat that?
2. Could you help me find a book?
3. Can you tell me how I can apply for a job on campus?
4. How can I make an appointment to meet with a counselor?
5. What is a *discussion section*?
6. What does *apply yourself* mean?
7. Could you tell me what happened in class yesterday?
8. Is there any meat in the soup?
9. Do you know where there is an ATM?
10. Can you tell me where the nearest copy store is?

D. Getting Information

○ Go over the directions and the examples.
○ Have students write five questions about their class, neighborhood, or city.
○ Put students in small groups to discuss the questions.
○ Call on students to share questions with the class.

ANSWER KEY

Answers will vary.

PART ③ THE MECHANICS OF LISTENING AND SPEAKING, PAGES 30–34

LANGUAGE FUNCTION: Asking for Directions

○ Go over the information in the box.
○ Ask comprehension questions: *What modals can you use to ask for directions? When do you need to ask directions? What should you say before you ask a stranger a question?*

🎧 A. Following Directions

○ Go over the directions.
○ Remind students to begin at the place marked *You are here* on the map.
○ Have students write the letter of the correct places on the lines as you play the audio program.
○ Repeat the audio program if necessary.
○ Go over the answers with the class.

Audio Script

1. A: Excuse me. Can you tell me where the college library is?
B: Sure. Just go down a block. Make a left at the college entrance. It's right there on your right.
A: Thanks.
B: You're welcome.
2. A: Excuse me. Could you tell me how to get to a drugstore?
B: A drugstore. Um, sure. Go down First Street one block. Make a left on Gareth Avenue.
A: Left on Gareth. O.K.
B: Then go down Gareth three blocks. There's a drugstore on the corner of Fourth and Gareth.
A: Fourth and Gareth.
B: Right.
A: Thanks a lot.
B: Uh-huh.
3. A: Excuse me. Can you tell me where to find a bookstore?
B: The college bookstore?
A: No. Just a regular bookstore.

B: Well, go down College Drive two blocks and make a left. There's a bookstore across from the park—across from the college.
A: Thanks a lot.
B: No problem.
4. A: Excuse me. Could you tell me where to find a bank?
B: Uh, yeah. Go down College Drive two blocks . . .
A: Two blocks . . .
B: Yeah. Then make a right on Third Street. Go about a block, a block and a half. There's a bank in the middle of the block. On Third.
A: Thanks.
B: Uh-huh.
5. A: Excuse me. Can you tell me how to get to the Career Planning Office at the college?
B: Sure. Go down College Drive to the entrance. Turn left. Go past the Admissions Building. Make another left on Valley Walk. Career Planning is across from Admissions.
A: On the corner of Campus Way and Valley Walk?
B: That's right.
A: Well, thanks.
B: You're welcome.

ANSWER KEY

1. C; 2. D; 3. E; 4. B; 5. A

EXPANSION ACTIVITY: Pair Work

○ Put students in pairs to take turns asking for and giving directions using the map.
○ Walk around the room to monitor the activity and provide help as needed.

🎧 INTONATION: Understanding Interjections

○ Go over the information in the box.
○ Ask comprehension questions: *What are interjections? When do we use them? Why are they important?*

TOEFL® iBT Tip

TOEFL iBT Tip 3: On the TOEFL iBT, students will hear speech that is realistic and natural, with varying intonation patterns. They will need to understand and effectively use stress, intonation, and pauses on both the listening and speaking parts of the test.

○ Point out that speakers in lectures and conversations on the test will often use interjections to indicate comprehension, surprise, a need for clarification, disappointment, and a variety of other emotions.

○ The ability to understand the use of interjections in American English will help the students in speaking tasks on the test and make them sound more "native-like."

ANSWER KEY

Conversation	Second Person's Meaning				
Person	Yes	No	You're welcome.	What?/ Pardon?	There's a problem!
1				✔	
2	✔				
3		✔			
4					✔
5		✔			
6	✔				

C. Using Interjections
○ Go over the directions and the example.
○ Model the activity. Read the first three questions and statements and elicit an interjection from a student in response.
○ Put students in pairs to practice the activity. Tell one student to be Student A and one to be Student B. You can have students switch roles for more practice. Walk around the room to monitor the activity and provide help as needed.

B. Understanding Interjections
○ Go over the directions.
○ Have students check the boxes on the chart as you play the audio program. Repeat if necessary.
○ Go over the answers with the class.

Audio Script
1. **A:** It's in the College Library.
   B: Huh?
2. **A:** Do you mean, "Try to enjoy your classes"?
   B: Uh-huh.
3. **A:** I think the test is tomorrow.
   B: Uh-uh.
4. **A:** I think the test is tomorrow.
   B: Uh-oh.
5. **A:** Thanks for all your help.
   B: Uh-huh.
6. **A:** Do you like it?
   B: Uh-huh.

EXPANSION ACTIVITY: That Means *No*
○ Put students in groups of three. Designate one as Student A, one as Student B, and one as the interpreter.
○ Model the activity. Have two students play the roles of A and B from Activity C. For example, Student A will say *Could I borrow your pencil?* Student B will respond with an interjection (e.g., *uh-uh*). You are the interpreter. You will interpret Student B's response (e.g., *that means* no).
○ Have students practice interjections in the groups of three.

PRONUNCIATION: /θ/ vs. /s/
○ Go over the information in the box.
○ Ask comprehension questions: *How do we make the /θ/ sound? Why is this sound important?*

D. Repeating Words with /θ/ and /s/
○ Go over the directions.
○ Play the audio program and have students repeat.

Audio Script
thank; sank; thick; sick; thaw; saw; path; pass; tenth; tense

E. Hearing the Difference Between /θ/ and /s/
○ Go over the directions.
○ Have students circle the word they hear as you play the audio program.
○ Put students in pairs to compare answers.
○ Go over the answers with the class.

Audio Script
1. sank	5. path	9. theme
2. sings	6. worse	10. tense
3. thaw	7. force	11. eighth
4. thick	8. thigh	12. some

ANSWER KEY
1. sank; 2. sings; 3. thaw; 4. thick; 5. path; 6. worse; 7. force; 8. thigh; 9. theme; 10. tense; 11. eighth; 12. some

EXPANSION ACTIVITY: Pronunciation Bingo
○ Have students create 4 x 4 grids for a Bingo game.
○ Ask students to choose 16 of the words in Exercise E and write one in each of the squares of the Bingo grid.
○ Have students mark off the words they hear on their grids and to call out *Bingo* when they have four in a row.
○ Call out words from Exercise E in random order.
○ When a student calls out Bingo, ask the student to read out each of the words in the line for the class to check.

F. Pronouncing /θ/ and /s/ in Conversations
○ Go over the directions.
○ Have students listen as you play the audio program.
○ Play the audio program a second time and have students repeat.

WORDS IN PHRASES: Expressions for Giving Directions
○ Go over the information in the box.
○ Ask comprehension questions: *What is another way to say* turn right? (make a right) *What is a* block? (a group of buildings)

G. Information Gap: Words in Phrases
○ Go over the directions.
○ Put students in pairs. Have Student A in each pair turn to page 201 and Student B turn to page 205.
○ Have students practice asking for locations of buildings on the map.
○ Have students check their answers with their partners.

ANSWER KEY
Answers may vary.
a. on Tenth Street, fourth from the corner
b. on Gareth Avenue, third from the corner
c. on Tenth Street, third from the corner
d. on Gareth Avenue, sixth from the corner
e. on Tenth Street, fifth from the corner
f. on Tenth Street, second from the corner
g. on Gareth Avenue, fourth from the corner
h. on Gareth Avenue, fifth from the corner

Put It Together

CRITICAL THINKING SKILL: Synthesizing
○ Being able to put together or synthesize skills and information is an important skill in second language learning.
○ Point out that in the activity *Asking for and Giving Directions*, students will use what they have learned in Part 3.

A. Asking For and Giving Directions

○ Go over the directions.
○ Direct students to the map on page 31.
○ Put students in pairs to practice asking for and giving directions.
○ Call on students to ask for and give directions.

B. Talking about Your Neighborhood

○ Go over the directions.
○ Put students in pairs to practice asking for and giving directions to places near your school.
○ Have students draw maps of their neighborhoods.
○ Have students use their maps to practice asking for and giving directions to places in their neighborhoods.

PART ④ BROADCAST ENGLISH
COLLEGE TODAY, PAGES 35–41

Before Listening
A. Thinking Ahead

○ Go over the directions.
○ Have students discuss the questions and write their answers in the chart.
○ Call on students to share their ideas with the class.

ANSWER KEY

Answers will vary.

B. Vocabulary Preparation

○ Go over the directions and questions.
○ Have students write the words or phrases on the lines and then compare answers with a partner.
○ Go over the answers with the class.

ANSWER KEY

1. majority; 2. appeals to you; 3. higher education;
4. seek out; 5. quarters; 6. Roughly; 7. dropping out;
8. joy; 9. percent; 10. experimenting

EXPANSION ACTIVITY: Beanbag Toss

○ Tell students they have one minute to review the vocabulary in Activity B.
○ After one minute, ask students to close their books.
○ Tell students that you will call on a student and toss a beanbag or ball. You will say one of the definitions, and the students should respond with the vocabulary word or phrase and throw the beanbag back.
○ Call on a student and toss the beanbag, saying *go and find*. Elicit an answer (*seek*) from the student and have them toss the beanbag or ball back to you.
○ Repeat with other students until all have a chance to participate. This is a fast-paced activity.

Listening
LISTENING STRATEGY: Understanding the Medial *T*

○ Go over the information in the box.
○ Ask questions: *What is a medial* T? *What does it sometimes sound like? How does the* T *sound different in the words* thirteen *and* thirty?

Pronunciation Note

○ Remind students that the stress pattern for numbers ending in –*teen* is different from numbers ending in –*ty*. For numbers ending in –*teen*, the second syllable is stressed like the first syllable. For numbers ending in –*ty*, the second syllable is unstressed.

○ A. Hearing the Medial *T*

○ Go over the directions.
○ Have students circle the numbers they hear as you play the audio program.
○ Go over the answers with the students.

Audio Script

1. 30	**8.** 13
2. 40	**9.** 40
3. 15	**10.** 15
4. 60	**11.** 60
5. 17	**12.** 70
6. 18	**13.** 18
7. 19	**14.** 90

ANSWER KEY

1. 30; 2. 40; 3. 15; 4. 60; 5. 17; 6. 18; 7. 19; 8. 13; 9. 40; 10. 15; 11. 60; 12. 70; 13. 18; 14. 90

B. Hearing the Medial *T* in Sentences

○ Go over the directions.
○ Have students write the numbers on the lines as you play the audio program.
○ Go over the answers with the class.

Audio Script

1. Almost 50 percent of the class can speak another language.
2. William started college when he was 40.
3. Roughly 30 percent of all high school graduates went to college.
4. They moved to Kenya when she was 14.
5. The average age is 13.
6. Many students lived in dormitories 50 years ago.
7. Becky graduated 15 years ago.
8. Ethan got married when he was 90.
9. Ashley moved into a dormitory when she was 17.
10. A person who is 30 or 40 can enjoy college more than someone who is 18 or 19.

ANSWER KEY

1. 50; 2. 40; 3. 30; 4. 14; 5. 13; 6. 50; 7. 15; 8. 90; 9. 17; 10. 30, 40, 18, 19

C. Hearing the Medial *T* Followed by /N/

○ Go over the directions.
○ Have students write the words on the lines as you play the audio program.
○ Go over the answers with the class.

Audio Script

1. I was bitten by some insect yesterday.
2. Do you know where I can find a drinking fountain?
3. I bought a blue cotton shirt.
4. Are you certain of that?
5. I have a mountain of homework tonight.

ANSWER KEY

1. bitten; 2. fountain; 3. cotton; 4. certain; 5. mountain

D. Listening for the Main Idea: Section 1

○ Go over the directions and the question.
○ Have students fill in the bubble as you play Section 1 of the audio program.
○ Go over the answer with the class.

Audio Script

Penkava: Arthur Levine, talk to us a bit about this historically. Has, has there been a marked change in how we approach higher education over, say, the last 50 years?

Levine: Oh, sure. Uh, college is real different these days. Fifty years ago we had, oh, roughly 15 percent of all high school graduates going to college. We're now up to 65 percent of all high school graduates. So it's become a rite of passage. What we're finding now is 50 years ago the majority of college students would have been men. A majority are now women. Fifty years ago, a majority of college students would have been 18 to 22; the average age is now over 25. Fifty years ago, the average college student would have been white; today a third of all college—20-odd percent of all college students are of color. Uh, fifty years ago, a majority—almost all—college students would have been full-time; today 42 percent are part-time. So it's a very different mix of people we're going to see on campus these days.

ANSWER KEY
A

LISTENING STRATEGY: Taking Notes: Using a Graphic Organizer
○ Go over the information in the box.
○ Ask questions: *How is a graphic organizer helpful for taking notes? When is a T-chart useful?*

E. Taking Notes: Using a Graphic Organizer
○ Go over the directions and the information on the graphic organizer.
○ Have students take notes on the T-chart as you play the audio program.
○ Have students compare ideas with a partner.
○ Go over the answers with the class.

Audio Script
Use the script for Activity D on page 18 of the Teacher's Edition.

ANSWER KEY

	50 Years Ago	Today
High School graduates going to college	15%	65%
Men/Women	Majority men	Majority women
Average age	18–22	over 25
Ethnicity (groups of people)	White	About a third people of color
Full-time/Part-time	Majority full-time	42% part-time

F. Listening for the Main Idea: Section 2
○ Go over the directions and the question.
○ Have students fill in the bubble as you play Section 2 of the audio program.
○ Go over the answer with the class.

Audio Script
Penkava: Well, Anne Matthews, what advice would you offer somebody so that there'd be a greater chance that something would click in their mind when they were in that lab, when they were in that class, so that—that they could gain something from this, from their college years, Anne Matthews.
Matthews: Oh, I would—I—I'd have a couple of piece of ad—pieces of advice. I'd say, take enough quarters for laundry. Talk to strangers, because this is the big chance to meet people very unlike you. I would say talk to professors, go to office hours. If you find a class that appeals to you, even ask them for extra reading. They'll—they'll kiss your feet in amazement and joy. I would say try everything, you know, Thai dance, botany, South American history—'cause no one cares if you turn out to be not any good at it. You know, you're in college and you're supposed to be experimenting. And my last piece of advice to a student on the younger end of the range, uh, the 17- or 18-year-old, would be: think about dropping out—because very often those years of 18, 19, and 20, uh, campuses are forced to do a lot more babysitting than they probably should. It's people who are 20, 30, 40 that really enjoy and get a great deal out of the undergraduate investment.

ANSWER KEY
A

G. Listening for Numbers
○ Go over the directions.
○ Have students write the numbers on the lines as you play the audio program. Repeat if necessary.
○ Have students check their answers in pairs.
○ Go over the answers with the class.

Audio Script

Matthews: And my last piece of advice to a student on the younger end of the range, the 17- or 18-year-old, would be: think about dropping out—because very often those years of 18, 19, and 20, uh, campuses are forced to do a lot more babysitting than they probably should. It's people who are 20, 30, 40 that really enjoy and get a great deal out of the undergraduate investment.

ANSWER KEY

And my last piece of advice to a student on the younger end of the range, the <u>17</u>- or <u>18</u>-year-old, would be: think about dropping out—because very often those years of <u>18</u>, <u>19</u>, and 20, uh, campuses are forced to do a lot more babysitting than they probably should. It's people who are 20, <u>30</u>, <u>40</u> that really enjoy and get a great deal out of the undergraduate investment.

LISTENING STRATEGY: Listening for Details

○ Go over the information in the box.
○ Ask questions: *Why are details important? What type of information might be a supporting detail?*

H. Listening for Details

○ Go over the directions.
○ Have students write the examples as you play the audio program.
○ Go over the answers with the class.

Audio Script

Matthews: I would say try everything, you know, Thai dance, botany, South American history—'cause no one cares if you turn out to be not any good at it. You know, you're in college and you're supposed to be experimenting.

ANSWER KEY

I would say try everything, you know, <u>Thai dance</u>, <u>botany</u>, South American <u>history</u>—'cause no one cares if you turn out to be not any good at it. You know, you're in college and you're supposed to be experimenting.

I. Listening for the Main Idea: Section 3

○ Go over the directions and the question.
○ Have students answer the question as you play the audio program.
○ Go over the answer with the class.

Audio Script

Penkava: 1-800-989-8255. 1-800-989-TALK. Jeff in Pullman, Washington. Hi there, Jeff.
Caller: Hi. Um, I'm a graduate student and a T.A., so I thought I could make a couple more suggestions that might be helpful.
Penkava: Sure.
Caller: Um, first off, um, it is good to seek out professors. And uh, I would also add that it's good to talk to your teaching assistants—they oftentimes have a little more time available, and they're generally pretty excited and want to work with students.
Penkava: Mm-hmm.
Caller: And the other suggestion I would make is, um, not to worry too much about grades the first couple of years, you know. Bs are good enough. But try to take the time to explore the material and uh, enjoy yourself, at least the first couple of years.
Penkava: Well, Jeff, thanks for your advice.
Caller: Thank you.

ANSWER KEY

Jeff is a graduate student and T.A. in Pullman, Washington.

TOEFL® iBT Tip

TOEFL iBT Tip 4: The TOEFL iBT measures the ability to understand the main idea or purpose and the important details of a conversation or a lecture.

○ Point out that the *Listening for Details* activity will help students improve their overall basic comprehension skills for the TOEFL iBT.

○ On the TOEFL iBT a main idea or detail question may appear in the following formats:
What are the speakers mainly discussing?
Why does the student want to talk to his professor?

J. Listening for Details
○ Go over the directions and the questions.
○ Have students answer the questions as you play the audio program.
○ Go over the answers with the class.

Audio Script
Use the script for Activity I on page 20 of the Teacher's Edition.

ANSWER KEY
1. professors; 2. teaching assistants; 3. grades;
4. explore the material and enjoy themselves

After Listening
A. Discussion
○ Go over the directions and the questions.
○ Put students in small groups to discuss the questions.
○ Call on students to share their ideas with the class.

EXPANSION ACTIVITY: Advice Column
○ Have students write a letter asking for advice about starting college.

○ Collect the letters and redistribute them so each student has another student's letter. Alternatively, put students in pairs to exchange letters.
○ Have students write responses to the letters they received. Encourage students to use ideas from the chapter as well as their own ideas in their responses.

CRITICAL THINKING STRATEGY: Recognizing Literal and Figurative Meanings
○ Go over the information in the box.
○ Ask comprehension questions: *What is a literal meaning? What is a figurative meaning? What can you do to try to understand a figurative meaning?*

B. Recognizing Literal and Figurative Meanings
○ Go over the directions and the questions.
○ Put students in pairs or small groups to discuss the questions.
○ Call on students to share their ideas with the class.

ANSWER KEY
Answers will vary.
1. Students might not know how to do laundry in pay machines.
2. They will be very happy with you.

C. Taking a Survey
○ Go over the directions and the questions.
○ Instruct students to talk with three or four English speakers and write their answers in the chart.
○ Put students in pairs to compare charts.

ANSWER KEY
Answers will vary.

D. Discussing Survey Results
○ Go over the directions.
○ Call on students to share what they learned with the class. In a large class, you may want to put students in small groups to discuss the results first.

PART 5 ACADEMIC ENGLISH
KEYS TO ACADEMIC SUCCESS, PAGES 42–50

Before Listening
A. Thinking Ahead
○ Go over the directions.
○ Have students write the advice that they expect the counselor to give.
○ Put students in pairs to compare ideas.
○ Call on students to share their ideas with the class.

ANSWER KEY
Answers will vary.

B. Vocabulary Preparation
○ Go over the directions.
○ Have students fill in the bubbles and then compare answers with a partner.
○ Go over the answers with the class.

ANSWER KEY
1. B; 2. C; 3. B; 4. A; 5. B; 6. C

EXPANSION ACTIVITY: Original Sentences
○ Have students write original sentences using the vocabulary words.
○ Put students in pairs to compare sentences.
○ Call on students to read their sentences to the class.

LISTENING STRATEGY: Taking Lecture Notes: Using an Outline
○ Go over the information in the box.
○ Ask questions: *How can you make an informal outline? What is the difference between a formal and an informal outline?*
○ Elicit answers to the questions at the bottom of the outline.

TOEFL® iBT Tip

TOEFL iBT Tip 5: Because the TOEFL iBT now allows note-taking, students need to learn the best strategies to take notes quickly and effectively.

○ Remind students that the listening strategy *Taking Lecture Notes: Outlining* can help them to find information for responses to reading and speaking questions as well as to develop a better written response.

○ Point out that putting notes into a graphic organizer can help students to make connections between the major and minor points in a lecture or conversation and enhance their ability to synthesize information between sources in preparation for the integrated tasks on the TOEFL iBT.

C. Taking Notes: Using an Outline
○ Go over the directions and the steps.
○ Have students work in pairs to create an outline for the items.
○ Have each pair compare outlines with another pair.
○ Go over the outline with the class. You may want to recreate the outline on the board or on an overhead transparency.

Culture Note
○ Labs are considered college services because they are resources provided to help students succeed in school. Clubs, on the other hand, are considered activities because their main purpose is recreation, although they may also help students with academics.

ANSWER KEY

I. University Library System	gen
A. Research Library	L
B. Undergraduate Library	L
C. Engineering Library	L
D. Art Library	L
E. Medical Library	L

ANSWER KEY, continued

II.	Services	*gen*
	A. Student Health Clinic	*S*
	B. Career Planning Office	*S*
	C. Labs	*S, gen*
	1. Language Lab	*S*
	2. Mathematics Lab	*S*
	3. Writing Lab	*S*
	D. Lecture Note Service	*S*
	E. ATMs	*S*
	F. Child Care Center	*S*
III.	Activities	*gen*
	A. Sports	*A, gen*
	1. Tennis	*A*
	2. Basketball	*A*
	3. Soccer	*A*
	4. Football	*A*
	5. Swimming	*A*
	B. Clubs	*A, gen*
	1. Chess Club	*A*
	2. International Student Club	*A*
	3. Ski Club	*A*
	4. Karate Club	*A*

Note: In this outline, it is important that the items go under the right heading, but the order of items under that heading is not important. For example, *Research Library* and *Art Library* must both be under *University Library System*, but it is not important that *Research Library* comes before *Art Library*.

Listening

LISTENING STRATEGY: Understanding New Words

○ Go over the information in the box.
○ Ask: *When do professors often give the definition of a new word? What expressions should you listen for?*

🎧 A. Understanding New Words

○ Go over the directions.
○ Have students write the definitions as you play the audio program.
○ Go over the answers with the class.

TOEFL® iBT Tip

TOEFL iBT Tip 6: The listening section of the TOEFL iBT checks comprehension of vocabulary words in the context of the topic and information presented in the lecture or conversation.

○ Point out that the listening strategy *Understanding New Words* will help students identify words or terms that are new or unfamiliar.

○ When speakers on the test define words in a conversation or lecture, it is likely that the concept or word will be presented in question format to check for understanding.

Audio Script

1. In this lecture, I'm going to discuss five keys to academic success for ESL students. Now, by the word *academic* I mean "college or university."
2. First, self-assessment. This is a process. In this process, you discover and understand four things about yourself.
3. In this process, you discover and understand four things about yourself: your interests (things that you like to do), your skills (things that you do well), your values (things that you believe in), and your personality.
4. In this process, you discover and understand four things about yourself: your interests (things that you like to do), your skills (things that you do well), your values (things that you believe in), and your personality.
5. Transition is the process of moving from college to the world of work.

ANSWER KEY

1. college or university; 2. process in which you discover and understand four things about yourself; 3. the things you do well; 4. the things you believe in; 5. the process of moving from college to the world of work (Note that this answer is specific to the context, not a general definition of the word.)

EXPANSION ACTIVITY: Do It Yourself

○ Model the activity. Choose a vocabulary word from this chapter (see box on page 7 of the Teacher's Edition) and use it in a sentence, followed by a definition (e.g., *The other day I went to a workshop. This is a special class for teachers on how to teach grammar.*).

○ Have students choose three new vocabulary words or phrases from the chapter and write sentences and then use the expressions from the strategy box.

○ Put students in pairs to read their sentences.

LISTENING STRATEGY: Organizing Your Notes: Paying Attention to Signposts

○ Go over the directions. Point out or elicit the difference between a literal signpost (e.g., *New York City – 244 miles*) and a figurative signpost (i.e., a signal that certain information is going to follow).

○ Ask: *What is a signpost? What are some examples of signposts? What should you do when you hear one?*

B. Taking Notes: Using an Outline

○ Go over the directions.

○ Have students fill in the outline as you play the audio program.

○ Put students in pairs to compare their outlines.

○ Go over the answers with the class.

Audio Script

Section 1

Lecturer: O.K. Let's get started. Welcome to Valley College. I'm the director of the Career Office here at the college, and we want to help you to be successful in your classes here, um, both now and when you finish ESL and start all your other classes. In this workshop, I'm going to discuss five keys to academic success for ESL students. Now, by the word *academic* I mean "college or university." So what will make you a successful student here at Valley College?

First, self-assessment. This is a process. In this process, you discover and understand four things about yourself: your *interests* (things that you like to do), your *skills* (the things that you do well), your *values* (things that you believe in), and your *personality*. It's important to understand yourself very well so that you can make good choices about your major and your future career. The Counseling Office can give you a self-assessment test, or you can use a computerized self-assessment program at the Computer Lab or Career Office.

Now, the second key to academic success is setting a goal. A goal is a carefully planned purpose. What goal do you hope to reach this year, next year, in four years? Now, after you set your goal or goals, you need a plan of action. In other words, what steps are you going to take, what do you have to do, to reach your goal?

Section 2

Lecturer: The third key to college success is knowing the college culture and environment. Now, for ESL students, this is very, very important because ESL students often don't understand the system of higher education in the United States. And I can't emphasize this enough: you *absolutely must* become familiar with this college and what it offers. Now, how can you do this? Study a map of the college. Find out where the offices and services are. Study your college catalog. Read the explanations of the services at the college. Ask a lot of *questions*! Let me say this again: *ask a lot of questions.* It's important to know about your college. Why? Because you need to know where to go for help when you have a problem. Also, even when you *don't* have a problem, there are many services that can make your college life more fun, more enjoyable, richer.

Section 3

Lecturer: Now, the fourth key to success in college is developing academic skills. ESL students usually know that they have to study hard, right? But they often don't know *how* to "study hard." They might not have the skills. Here are just some of the skills that you need: First, you need to do all of the reading before you come to class each day. Second, you need to find key points in the reading and highlight them with a highlighter—yellow or orange or green. Next, you need to make notes on important new words and their definitions. Fourth, you need to take good lecture notes and write down any questions that you think of. Fifth, it's important to form a study group with a few students in each class. In this study group, you can review and compare your lecture notes.

Sixth, it is also important to make good use of academic services at the college. Here are three: Student Services offers special workshops on subjects such as note-taking and using your time well. The Math Lab has tutors who can give you individual help. The Writing Center also offers tutors who can help you with your essays and research.

Section 4

Lecturer: The fifth key to success is transition. Transition is the process of moving from college to the world of work. If you have a part-time job now, you've already started this process. Great. The best part-time job, of course, is one that gives you experience in your field of interest, in your major. Now, in addition, you need to visit us here at the Career Office at the college. It's here you can learn several things: how to write your résumé, how to look for a job, how to find careers that relate to your major, and how to prepare for a job interview. Then you're ready to move from school to work. O.K. Any questions?

ANSWER KEY

Keys to Academic Success

Section 1

Introduction

I. Self-assessment = <u>process in which you discover and understand four things about yourself</u>
   A. You can understand your:
      1. <u>interests</u>
      2. <u>skills</u>
      3. <u>values</u>
      4. <u>personality</u>
   B. Places to take a self-assessment test
      1. <u>Counseling Office</u>
      2. <u>Computer Lab</u>
      3. <u>Career Office</u>
II. Setting a goal
   A. Goals for different time periods
   B. Plan of action for your goal

Section 2

III. Knowing the College Culture and Environment
   A. How to learn about this
      1. Study <u>a map of the college</u>
      2. Find out <u>where the offices and services are</u>
      3. Study <u>your college catalog</u>
      4. Read <u>the explanations of the services at the college</u>
      5. <u>Ask a lot of questions</u>
   B. Important to know about your college because
      1. <u>You need to know where to go for help when you have a problem</u>
      2. <u>There are many services that can make your college life more fun</u>

Section 3

IV. Developing Academic Skills
   A. <u>Do all the reading before you come to class</u>
   B. <u>Find key points in the reading and highlight them with a highlighter</u>
   C. <u>Make notes on important new words and their definitions</u>
   D. <u>Take good lecture notes and write down questions</u>
   E. <u>Form a study group with other students to review and compare notes</u>
   F. <u>Make good use of academic services</u>
      1. Student Services: <u>workshops on note-taking and using time well</u>
      2. Math lab: <u>tutor</u>
      3. Writing Center: <u>tutor</u>

Section 4

V. Transition to the World of Work
   A. Part-time job
   B. <u>Career Office</u>
      1. <u>Learn to write a résumé</u>
      2. <u>Learn how to look for a job</u>
      3. <u>Learn how to find careers that relate to your major</u>
      4. <u>Learn how to prepare for a job interview</u>

🎧 C. Checking Your Notes

- ○ Go over the directions, the question, and the bulleted points.
- ○ Have students put a star next to the most important key as you play the audio program.

Audio Script

Use the script for Activity B on page 24 of the Teacher's Edition.

ANSWER KEY

Knowing the college culture and environment

After Listening
A. Using Your Notes
○ Go over the directions and the questions.
○ Have students discuss the questions in small groups.
○ Call on students to share their answers with the class.

ANSWER KEY
1. your interests, skills, values, and personality
2. at the Counseling Office, Computer Lab, or Career Office
3. Study a map of the college; find out where the offices and services are; study your college catalog; read the explanations of the services at the college; ask a lot of questions.
4. Knowing the college culture and environment; the speakers says it's very, very important, he can't emphasize it enough, they absolutely must become familiar, he repeats that they need to ask a lot of questions

B. Getting to Know a College Campus
○ Go over the directions.
○ Have students work in pairs to match the places to the situations.
○ Go over the answers with the class.

ANSWER KEY
1. d; 2. e; 3. f; 4. c; 5. b; 6. a; 7. h; 8. g; 9. i; 10. j

C. Making Connections
○ Go over the directions.
○ Have students work individually to list the advice they remember.
○ Have students share their lists and discuss the questions.
○ Call on students to share their ideas with the class.

ANSWER KEY
1. ask questions/talk to people; try different things; use time well
2. Answers will vary.
3. Answers will vary.

EXPANSION ACTIVITY: Rank the Advice
○ Have students rank the advice from Activity C in order of most useful (1) to least useful.
○ Put students in pairs to compare ideas.
○ Call on students to share their ideas with the class.

Put It All Together
○ Go over the directions. Have students read the steps.
○ **Step 1:** Have students choose two colleges or universities.
○ **Step 2:** Have students list questions about the schools.

EXPANSION ACTIVITY: Finding Information on a Website
○ Photocopy and distribute the worksheet *Finding Information on a Website* on page BLM 3.
○ Have students read the information and answer the questions.
○ Go over the answers with the class.

ANSWER KEY
1. Athletics; 2. Administration; 3. Class Schedule; 4. Financial Aid; 5. International Fashion Show; 6. New theater to open in spring; 7. Faculty/Staff

○ **Step 3:** Have each student explore the websites for the schools, looking for the answers to their questions and finding out interesting, special, or unusual features.
○ **Step 4:** Have students take notes on the T-chart with the information that they find on the websites.

SPEAKING STRATEGY: Asking for Clarification
○ Go over the information in the box.
○ Ask questions: *What do you need to be a good listener? How can you ask for clarification when you don't understand something?*

○ **Step 5:** Put students in pairs or small groups to share the information they learned. Have students take notes as their classmates are speaking. Walk around to monitor the activity and provide help as needed.

UNIT 1 BUSINESS

CHAPTER 2 THE GLOBAL ECONOMY

In Part 1, students will look at and discuss a magazine advertisement. In Part 2, students will listen to two people talking about products. In Part 4, students will listen to a radio interview about where T-shirts are made. In Part 5, students will listen to a lecture about a U.S. company's failure to break into the Japanese market. Finally, students will give a presentation on selling a new product.

VOCABULARY

acquaintances	dominate	manufacture	route
advertisement	effective	market	seed
beverage	flourish	marketer	segments
bucks	fruit pulp	marketing	stuff
cheap	generate a positive attitude toward	marketplace	target audience
consumer goods	global economy	nope	textile
cool	highly desirable trait	nutritious	thirst quenching
copy	industry	odd	whoa
curious	infrastructure	overseas	wild
customer traffic	keep track of	perfect	workforce
demand	labels	point-of-purchase displays	yeah
diversify	local	postmodern	

LISTENING STRATEGIES

Listening for Supporting Information
Identifying a Causal Chain
Listening for an Anecdote
Asking Questions

CRITICAL THINKING STRATEGIES

Previewing: Brainstorming (Part 2)
Separating Cause From Time (Part 4)
Making Connections (Part 4)
Note: Strategies in bold are highlighted in the Student Book.

MECHANICS OF LISTENING AND SPEAKING

Intonation: *Wh–* Questions
Language Functions: Greeting People You Know
   Responding to Greetings: General
   Returning Greetings
   Responding to Greetings: Specific
Pronunciation: Reduced Forms of Words
Words In Phrases: Expressions with *Look, Seem,* and *Sound* + Adjective

SPEAKING STRATEGIES

Outlining
Making Eye Contact

TEST-TAKING STRATEGY

Making Predictions

CHAPTER 2 The Global Economy

Chapter 2 Opener, page 51

○ Direct students' attention to the photo and chapter title. Go over the directions and questions.
○ Put students in pairs to share their ideas.
○ Call on students to share their ideas with the class.

PART ① INTRODUCTION
ADVERTISING MESSAGES, PAGES 52–53

A. Thinking Ahead

○ Direct students' attention to the photos. Ask: *What products do you see?*
○ Go over the directions and the questions.
○ Put students in small groups to discuss the questions.
○ Call on students to share their ideas with the class.

ANSWER KEY
Answers will vary.

Culture Notes

○ McDonalds is a chain of restaurants that was begun in the United States but is now seen all over the world. The company's symbols are the familiar "golden arches" logo and the clown character Ronald McDonald.
○ The "swoosh" logo is the symbol of Nike, an American company that makes shoes and sportswear—clothes for sports. Nike hires famous athletes to promote its slogan: "Just do it."
○ Motorola, another American company, is the world's second-biggest maker of mobile phones. The company also makes wireless networks and broadband computer equipment.
○ HSBC is a banking and financial services organization. HSBC's headquarters are in England, but the company has offices in 77 countries and territories in Europe, the Asia-Pacific region, the Americas, the Middle East, and Africa.

EXPANSION ACTIVITY: Ad Descriptions

○ Bring in print ads from newspapers or magazines, or have students bring them in.
○ Make sure each student has an ad to work with.
○ Have students write three sentences describing the ad.
○ Put students in small groups. Have one student in each group collect the ads and another student collect the descriptions.
○ Assign one student in each group to read the descriptions aloud, and have the group match each description with the correct ad.

B. Studying an Ad

○ Direct students' attention to the ad on page 53.
○ Go over the directions and the questions.
○ Have students read the ad and discuss the questions in small groups.

ANSWER KEY
The ad is for clothing from the United States. This clothing can be bought in many countries around the world both in Ralph Lauren's own stores and in most department stores, such as Macy's in the U.S.

Culture Notes

○ *Polo Ralph Lauren* is an American brand of clothing created by the designer Ralph Lauren. Lauren was born with the last name Lipschitz; his parents were immigrants to New York City. He changed his name to sound less like an immigrant, and more like the traditional upper-class families he admired.
○ Polo is a sport played on horseback. In America, it is usually played only by wealthy people.
○ Some students may recognize Ralph Lauren's name from the TV show *Friends,* on which he played the character Rachel's boss.

C. Discussion
○ Go over the directions.
○ Put students in pairs to discuss the questions.
○ Call on students to share their ideas with the class.

ANSWER KEY
Answers will vary.

D. Journal Writing
○ Go over the directions.
○ Explain that this is a freewriting activity and does not have to be perfect. Point out that journal writing can be a warm-up to a more structured writing assignment, helping to generate ideas.
○ Set a time limit of five minutes.
○ Put students in pairs to read or talk about their writing.

PART ② SOCIAL LANGUAGE
STUFF MADE OVERSEAS, PAGES 54–58

Before Listening
CRITICAL THINKING STRATEGY: Previewing: Brainstorming
○ Go over the information in the box.
○ Ask comprehension questions: *What is brainstorming? Why is it a good idea to brainstorm before you listen?*

A. Brainstorming
○ Go over the directions. Make sure students understand what labels are and how to find where an object is made.
○ Have students complete the chart with objects and where each is made.

ANSWER KEY
Answers will vary.

B. Discussion
○ Go over the directions and the questions.
○ Have students discuss the questions in small groups.
○ Call on students to share their ideas with the class.

ANSWER KEY
Answers will vary.

C. Vocabulary Preparation
○ Go over the directions. Ask volunteers to read the conversations to the class.
○ Have students match the definitions with the words in red.
○ Go over the answers with the class.

ANSWER KEY
1. a; 2. e; 3. d; 4. c; 5. g; 6. b; 7. f

EXPANSION ACTIVITY: Create Conversations
○ Put students in pairs to create conversations using the informal words from Activity C.
○ Instruct students to write a conversation of at least six sentences. They can write about one of the following topics or their own ideas: *the best places to meet new friends; the hardest or most fun part of learning English; their favorite movie or sports stars.*
○ Call on pairs of students to perform their conversations for the class.

Listening
🎞️🎧 A. Listening for the Main Idea
○ Go over the directions and the questions.
○ Play the video or audio program.
○ Ask students: *What advice do most speakers give?*

Audio Script
Chrissy: Hey, Brandon. What's up? I *love* your glasses. Are they new?
Brandon: Yeah. I got them at that designer discount place downtown.

Chrissy: They are really cool. I'd like some like that. Who made them?

Brandon: It says "Olivier Renaud." Sounds French. Nope, wait a minute. It says "Made in China. "

Chrissy: Huh. That's like a lot of stuff these days. See these shoes?

Brandon: Yeah.

Chrissy: Don't they look cool?

Brandon: Nice.

Chrissy: Yeah, I thought they looked very fashionable, but if you look closely—

Brandon: Hey, they're plastic!

Chrissy: They're made in China, too, and—they were only 30 bucks!

Brandon: Cool.

Chrissy: Yeah. I noticed you can get great-looking copies of designer stuff that's made overseas. China, Korea—

Brandon: Hey, speaking of stuff made overseas, have you seen that new ad for Super Mints?

Chrissy: Um, I don't know.

Brandon: It's really wild. There are all these odd couples—an old lady and a little boy, a woman and her dog, two guys—and one wants to kiss the other.

Chrissy: Oh, yeah, but the other refuses because the one that wants a kiss has bad breath!

Brandon: Yeah, it's done in wild colors and settings, like a music video. I was so curious, I bought some. I noticed they're from England; I was wondering if the commercial is British, too. It just didn't look American.

Chrissy: I don't know. I think they remake commercials for the country they want to sell the product in 'cause you have to appeal to the local market. You've got to relate the product to local values.

Brandon: Yeah, and there's stuff you can do in commercials in other countries that you *sure* can't do here.

Chrissy: Hey, that's right! I saw this commercial in a movie theater last summer in France. It was just for yogurt, but they showed this woman's—

Brandon: Whoa, we're going to have to pick this up later. I'm going to be late for class.

Chrissy: All right. Hey, Brandon, what did you do with those Super Mints? You could use some!

Brandon: *Chrissy!*

ANSWER KEY

The students bought glasses, shoes, and Super Mints.

 B. Listening for Details

○ Go over the directions.
○ Have students complete the chart as you play the video or audio program a second time.
○ Put students in pairs to compare answers.
○ Go over the answers with the class.

Audio Script

Use the script for Activity A on page 29 of the Teacher's Edition.

ANSWER KEY

Objects	Country They Are From
Brandon's glasses	China
Chrissy's shoes	China
Brandon's Super Mints	England

C. Listening for Descriptive Language

○ Go over the directions.
○ Have students write their guesses on the lines as you play the video or audio program.
○ Go over the answers with the class.

Audio Script

Brandon: Hey, speaking of stuff made overseas, have you seen that new ad for Super Mints?

Chrissy: Um, I don't know.

Brandon: It's really wild. There are all these odd couples—an old lady and a little boy, a woman and her dog, two guys—and one wants to kiss the other.

Chrissy: Oh, yeah, but the other refuses because the one that wants a kiss has bad breath!

Brandon: Yeah, it's done in wild colors and settings, like a music video. I was so curious, I bought some. I noticed they're from England; I was wondering if the commercial is British, too. It just didn't look American.

Chrissy: I don't know. I think they remake commercials for the country they want to sell the product in 'cause you have to appeal to the local market. You've got to relate the product to local values.

Brandon: Yeah. And there's stuff you can do in commercials in other countries that you *sure* can't do here.

ANSWER KEY

1. wild; 2. odd; 3. old; 4. bad; 5. little; 6. wild; 7. curious; 8. British; 9. American; 10. local; 11. local

Grammar Notes

❍ Elicit or review where adjectives often appear in sentences: that is, before nouns and after verbs such as *be, seem,* and *look.*

❍ Point out the three adjective endings used for nationality (*–an, –ish, –ese*). Elicit other examples with these endings (e.g., *Canadian, Indian, Mexican, Polish, Irish, Japanese*).

TOEFL® iBT Tip

TOEFL iBT Tip 1: The TOEFL iBT tests the ability to understand details of a lecture or conversation.

❍ Point out that the activity *Listening for Descriptive Language* will help students to improve their understanding of inference, fact and detail, and general listening comprehension questions.

❍ A better understanding of descriptive language can also be applied to the integrated listening-reading-speaking and reading-listening-writing tasks.

EXPANSION ACTIVITY: Very Short Stories

❍ Have students use all the words in the box for Activity C in a single sentence. Tell students they have to write about a situation that is different from the one in the audio program.

❍ Have students read their sentences to the class.

❍ Vote on whose sentence is the best.

LISTENING STRATEGY: Listening for Supporting Information

❍ Go over the information in the box.

❍ Ask comprehension questions: *When do people often give support? What word do you sometimes hear before supporting information? Does this word always come before the supporting information?*

D. Listening for Supporting Information

❍ Go over the directions.

❍ Have students write their answers on the lines as you play the video or audio program.

❍ Have students check their answers in pairs.

❍ Go over the answers with the class.

Audio Script

Use the script for Activity C on page 30 of the Teacher's Edition.

ANSWER KEY

1. It has odd couples and wild colors and settings like a music video.
2. You have to appeal to the local market and relate the product to local values.

After Listening

A. Information Gap

❍ Go over the directions and the questions.

❍ Put students in pairs. Have Student A in each pair turn to page 202 and Student B turn to page 206.

❍ Have students ask their partner questions to complete the catalog page.

❍ If necessary, go over the answers with the class.

ANSWER KEY

Parma Ham: Imported from Italy; 20 lbs.; $165.00
Fancy Arare Crackers: Made in Japan; 1 lb.; $25.00
Smoked Salmon: Flown in from Scotland; 2 lbs.; $35.00
Coffee Beans: Imported from Columbia; 5 1-lb. bags; $50.00

B. Taking a Survey

○ Go over the directions and the example.
○ You may want to reproduce the chart on the board. Model the activity. Call on a student and ask the four questions in the chart. Write the student's answers on the board.
○ Go over the questions on the chart. Have students write a question in the bottom row of the chart.
○ Have students interview three classmates and write the answers on the chart.

ANSWER KEY

Answers will vary.

C. Discussing Survey Results

○ Go over the directions and the questions.
○ Have students form groups of five, trying not to be in groups with classmates they interviewed.
○ Have students discuss the questions in their groups.
○ Call on students to share their ideas with the class.

ANSWER KEY

Answers will vary.

EXPANSION ACTIVITY: Team Challenge

○ Divide the class into teams.
○ Have each team brainstorm the names of companies in different countries. You may want to suggest countries (China, Korea, Japan, the U.S., Germany, Italy), or have students generate their own list.
○ Say the name of a country. Have each team take turns naming one company from that country. Each country named earns a point for that team.

○ Continue with other countries, allowing the teams to rotate being the first to answer.

PART ❸ THE MECHANICS OF LISTENING AND SPEAKING, PAGES 59–65

🎧 INTONATION: *Wh–* Questions

○ Go over the information in the box. Play the audio program.
○ Ask comprehension questions: *What are wh– words? Does your voice go up or down at the end of these questions? How is the intonation different from* yes/no *questions?*

🎧 A. Asking *Wh–* Questions

○ Go over the directions.
○ Have students listen and repeat the *wh–* questions in the box as you play the audio program.

B. Asking and Answering *Wh–* Questions

○ Go over the directions and the example.
○ Have students take turns asking and answering six *wh–* questions with a partner.
○ Walk around to monitor the activity and provide help as needed. Make sure students are using the correct intonation.

LANGUAGE FUNCTIONS: Greeting People You Know

○ Go over the information in the box.
○ Ask questions: *What is an informal way to greet people you know? Which way do you think is more formal? What are some answers to a* how *question? What are some ways to answer a* wh– *question?*

🎧 C. Greeting People You Know

○ Go over the directions.
○ Have students write the words they hear as you play the audio program.
○ Go over the answers with the class.

Audio Script

1. **A:** Hi! What's up?
   B: Oh, nothing much.
2. **A:** Hi. How's it going?
   B: Great!
3. **A:** Hi. How have you been?
   B: Not bad.
4. **A:** Hi. How are you?
   B: Hi! Just great.
5. **A:** Hi. What have you been up to lately?
   B: I've been really busy studying.

ANSWER KEY

1. What's up? 2. Great! 3. How have you been? 4. Hi! Just great. 5. been up to; I've been really busy studying.

Responding to Greetings: General

○ Go over the information in the box.
○ Ask comprehension questions: *How can you answer the question* How are you? *How can you answer* What's new?

D. Responding to Greetings: General

○ Go over the directions.
○ Have students circle the best answer to the greeting they hear as you play the audio program.
○ Put students in pairs to compare answers.
○ Go over the answers with the class.

Audio Script

1. How are you?
2. How's it going?
3. What did you do last night?
4. What's up?
5. How are you doing?
6. What's new?

ANSWER KEY

1. Fine. 2. Not bad. 3. Nothing much. 4. Nothing.
5. Fine. 6. Not much.

Returning Greetings

○ Go over the information in the box.
○ Ask comprehension questions: *Why do we return greetings? What is a common way to repeat a greeting question?*

E. Returning Greetings

○ Go over the directions.
○ Have students complete the conversation, using expressions in the box.
○ Have students compare conversations in pairs.
○ Call on pairs of volunteers to repeat their conversations to the class.

ANSWER KEY

A: Hi, Bob.
B: Hi, Annie. How <u>are you?</u>
A: I'm fine. <u>How about you?</u>
B: I'm fine, too. <u>What's new with you?</u>
A: Not much. What's <u>new with you?</u>
B: <u>Not much</u>

Responding to Greetings: Specific

○ Go over the information in the box. Play the audio program.
○ Ask comprehension questions: *Who do we often give specific answers to? Why?*

F. Responding to Greetings: Specific

○ Go over the directions and the example.
○ Put students in pairs to take turns greeting and responding. Remind students to switch roles after three greetings and responses.
○ Walk around to monitor the activity and make sure students are using correct intonation.
○ Call on volunteers to say the conversation in front of the class.

PRONUNCIATION: Reduced Forms of Words

○ Go over the information in the box. Play the audio program.
○ Ask questions: *What's the reduced form of* How are you doing? *What is the long form of* How 'boutchu?

TOEFL® iBT Tip

TOEFL iBT Tip 2: In the lectures and conversations on the TOEFL iBT students will hear speech that is realistic and natural in English and includes reductions. They will also need to produce intelligible speech and effectively use stress, intonation, and pauses in order to succeed on the speaking part of the test.

○ Point out that the pronunciation activity *Reduced Forms of Words* will help students understand speakers in the lectures and conversations on the test, who will often use reductions.

G. Reduced Forms of Words

○ Go over the directions.
○ Have students write the long forms of the reduced forms they hear as you play the audio program.
○ Go over the answers with the class.

Audio Script

A: Hi. Whasup?
B: Hi. Not much. Howzit going with you?
A: I dunno. I've been pretty busy lately. Whatuv you been up to?
B: I've been pretty busy, too. Howya doing in English?
A: Not bad, but it's a lotta work.

ANSWER KEY

1. What's up; 2. How is it; 3. don't know; 4. What have; 5. How are you; 6. a lot of

---

EXPANSION ACTIVITY: Dictation

○ Tell students you are going to dictate five sentences.
○ Have students write the sentences you dictate. Say each sentence three times. Create your own or use the ones below. Use reduced forms when you dictate.
How's it going at work?
What have you been up to at school lately?
How are you doing in English class?
I've been reading a lot of books.

○ Have students compare sentences with a partner.
○ Ask volunteers to write the sentences on the board.

WORDS IN PHRASES: Expressions with *Look, Seem,* and *Sound* + Adjective

○ Go over the information in the box.
○ Ask comprehension questions: *What verbs are often followed by adjectives? Can you use* sound + *adjective in a sentence?*

H. Words in Phrases

○ Go over the directions and the examples.
○ Model the activity with a student. Make comments to the student about what he or she is wearing and ask about what he or she did last weekend. Use *look, seem* and *sound* + adjective in your opinions.
○ Put students in pairs to take turns giving opinions with the expressions in the box.
○ Ask volunteers to say their conversations in front of the class.

Put It Together

A. Greeting Classmates

○ Go over the directions for the activity.
○ **Step 1:** Have students write eight things they have done this week on the lines.
○ **Step 2:** Divide the class into two teams.
○ Go over the examples in the box. Point out that students on Team A will greet Team B students first. Team B students will respond to the greeting. Team B students can give specific information using their Recent Activities lists. Encourage students on Team A to use *look, seem,* or *sound* + adjective in their responses to specific information.
○ Set a time limit of five minutes. Have Team A students greet and talk to Team B students. Remind Team A students to write down how many students they talk to.
○ After five minutes, have students exchange roles. Set a time limit of five minutes. Now Team B students will greet Team A students first. Again, remind Team B students to write down how many students they talk to.
○ Have each team total the number of people their members talked to. Ask for the totals from each team.

EXPANSION ACTIVITY: That Sounds Exciting!

○ Write five adjectives on the board: *exciting, boring, terrible, wonderful,* and *painful.*
○ Tell students that they are going to respond to someone's news with *That sounds* + one of the adjectives on the board.
○ Model the activity. Tell the class something you have done (e.g., *I had surgery last year*) and elicit a response (e.g., *That sounds painful*).
○ Have students write sentences about one experience for each adjective.
○ Call on students to read their sentences. Elicit responses from other students.

B. Talking about the Week

○ Go over the directions.
○ **Step 1:** Have students write their activities on the one-week agenda.
○ **Step 2:** Have students take turns greeting and responding with specific information from their agenda. Each student should speak at least twice.
○ Walk around to monitor the activity and provide help as needed.
○ Call on volunteers to say their conversation in front of the class.

PART ④ BROADCAST ENGLISH
THE TRAVELS OF A T-SHIRT, PAGES 66–70

Before Listening

A. Thinking Ahead

○ Go over the directions.
○ Have students discuss the questions in small groups.
○ Call on students to share their ideas with the class.

ANSWER KEY

Answers will vary.

B. Vocabulary Preparation

○ Go over the directions.
○ Have students write the words or phrases on the lines and then compare answers with a partner.
○ Go over the answers with the class.

ANSWER KEY

1. flourish; 2. perfect; 3. diversify; 4. dominate;
5. cheap; 6. postmodern; 7. manufacture; 8. textile;
9. workforce; 10. infrastructure

EXPANSION ACTIVITY: Beanbag Toss

○ Tell students they have one minute to review the vocabulary in Activity B.
○ After one minute, ask students to close their books.
○ Tell students that you will call on a student and toss a beanbag or ball. You will say one of the definitions, and the student should respond with the vocabulary word or phrase and throw the beanbag back.
○ Call on a student and toss the beanbag, saying *do well.* Elicit an answer from the student (*perfect*) and have them toss the beanbag or ball back to you.
○ Repeat with other students. This is a fast-paced activity.

TEST-TAKING STRATEGY: Making Predictions

○ Go over the information in the box.
○ Ask questions: *What do you do when you make predictions? Why should you do it?*

C. Making Predictions

○ Go over the directions.
○ Have students discuss the question in small groups.
○ Call on students to share their ideas with the class.

ANSWER KEY

Answers will vary.

TOEFL® iBT Tip

TOEFL iBT Tip 3: The lectures and conversations on the TOEFL iBT, as well as the reading and writing topics, will require students to anticipate the vocabulary and information that they might encounter on the test.

○ Point out that the *Making Predictions* activity will help students to activate their background knowledge and vocabulary about a specific topic and anticipate what the speaker might say.

○ Remind students that the ability to make predictions about a topic will also help them to maintain focus while listening to lectures.

Listening

🎧 A. Listening for the Main Idea

○ Go over the directions.
○ Have students write the answer to the question as you play the audio program.
○ Go over the answer with the students.

Audio Script

Siegel: There was a time not too long ago when most clothing bought in the U.S. was made in the U.S. No longer. Take T-shirts, for example. Most shirts on sale in American stores today come from such countries as Honduras, Vietnam, and, more and more often, China. Chinese companies have spent the last decade learning how to perfect the cheap manufacture of quality T-shirts. And with the expiration of apparel quotas, China is expected to dominate the world T-shirt market. This week we're running a series inspired by the book *The Travels of a T-shirt in the Global Economy* by Pietra Rivoli, a professor at Georgetown University. We asked her to show NPR's Adam Davidson around Shanghai, where many T-shirts are sewn.

Davidson: The Huangpu River, a tributary of the Yangtze, has been a cotton and textile water highway for almost a hundred years. Pietra Rivoli is on a boat looking out at Shanghai, China's busiest and fastest-growing city.

Rivoli: The cotton for a typical, uh, T-shirt that was made in China might have left west Texas, uh, and gone to California and then to Long Beach probably, the big port on our West Coast, and traveled all the way here.

Davidson: Much of the U.S. cotton arriving at the port of Shanghai is knit into cloth and then sewn into T-shirts, and this is exactly what Shanghai workers have been doing for most of the last hundred years: making T-shirts and other apparel. But things have been changing rapidly in recent decades. Shanghai has become the financial center of mainland China. Instead of cotton mills, the banks of the Huangpu are crowded now with exciting postmodern skyscrapers that house things like banks, ad agencies, hip restaurants, and absurdly expensive shops. The city has a newness and wealth that rivals New York, London, and Tokyo. Rivoli says none of this would be here, though, if the textile mills hadn't come first.

Rivoli: Because once you have one kind of factory, you can diversify into other kinds of factories, and your workforce gains skills, and you get this infrastructure that you see here that allows the ships to come in and out, and it allows trade to flourish. So it really started—what you see here today, which is really a fantastically modern city—was started by the investment of especially the British and the Japanese and the cotton factories that they built.

Davidson: As Chinese workers do better, though, there is a price to pay on the other side of the world. Greg Burgess used to work at one of the many T-shirt plants in Florence, Alabama. It closed a couple years ago. It couldn't compete with all those cheap Chinese imports. Burgess remembers the day he realized Florence's economy was in trouble.

Burgess: I was actually at Wal-Mart with my wife, and she was trying some clothes on. And I just walked over to a rack of shirts. There was, like, six shirts on this rack, and I just flipped through, and not one tag said 'Made in the USA.' And I knew then. And, I mean, these were from all different countries: Mexico, Sri Lanka, Dominican Republic, China. And I knew right then. I said, 'Not one shirt out of six in the U.S.' Then we knew it was time to start looking for something else.

ANSWER KEY

The textile mills made Shanghai a wealthy city.

🎧 B. Listening for Details
○ Go over the directions.
○ Have students follow the route on the map as you play the audio program and then answer the questions.
○ Go over the answers with the class.

Audio Script
Rivoli: The cotton for a typical, uh, T-shirt that was made in China might have left west Texas, uh, and gone to California and then to Long Beach probably, the big port on our West Coast, and traveled all the way here.

ANSWER KEY
1. west Texas; 2. California

LISTENING STRATEGY: Identifying a Causal Chain
○ Go over the information in the box.
○ Ask questions: *What is a cause? What words or expressions introduce causes?*

🎧 C. Identifying a Causal Chain
○ Go over the directions.
○ Have students write the causes in the graphic organizer as you play the audio program.
○ Go over the answers with the class.

Audio Script
Davidson: The city has a newness and wealth that rivals New York, London, and Tokyo. Rivoli says none of this would be here, though, if the textile mills hadn't come first.
Rivoli: Because once you have one kind of factory, you can diversify into other kinds of factories, and your workforce gains skills, and you get this infrastructure that you see here that allows the ships to come in and out, and it allows trade to flourish. So it really started—what you see here today, which is really a fantastically modern city—was started by the investment of especially the British and the Japanese and the cotton factories that they built.

ANSWER KEY

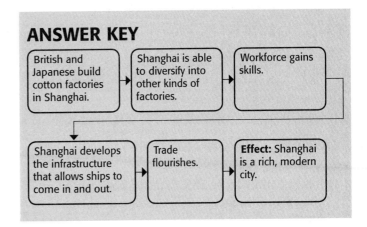

LISTENING STRATEGY: Listening for an Anecdote
○ Go over the information in the box.
○ Ask questions: *What is an anecdote? Why do people tell anecdotes in a discussion?*

🎧 D. Listening for an Anecdote
○ Go over the directions and the question.
○ Have students write the answer as you play the audio program.
○ Have students compare ideas with a partner.
○ Go over the answers with the class.

Audio Script
Davidson: As Chinese workers do better, though, there is a price to pay on the other side of the world. Greg Burgess used to work at one of the many T-shirt plants in Florence, Alabama. It closed a couple years ago. It couldn't compete with all those cheap Chinese imports. Burgess remembers the day he realized Florence's economy was in trouble.
Burgess: I was actually at Wal-Mart with my wife, and she was trying some clothes on. And I just walked over to a rack of shirts. There was, like, six shirts on this rack, and I just flipped through, and not one tag said 'Made in the USA.' And I knew then. And, I mean, these were from all different countries: Mexico, Sri Lanka, Dominican Republic, China. And I knew right then. I said, 'Not one shirt out of six in the U.S.' Then we knew it was time to start looking for something else.

ANSWER KEY

He was looking at shirts in Wal-Mart and noticed that none of them was made in the United States.

CRITICAL THINKING STRATEGY: Separating Cause from Time

○ It is important to be able to distinguish causal chains from events that simply happen close together in time.

○ Different words are used to express time relationships (e.g., *She quit her job* after *she got married.*) and causal ones (e.g., *She quit her job* because *she got married.*).

○ However, words for time are often used to imply a causal relationship. Listen carefully to context and the speaker's tone to understand the intended meaning. Students should ask, *Is evidence given for a causal relationship?*

EXPANSION ACTIVITY: Telling an Anecdote

○ Have students look back at the list of eight things they did in Put It Together Activity A on page 63.

○ Have them choose the most interesting thing on the list to write an anecdote about.

○ Have students write the anecdote in five complete sentences.

○ Put students in small groups to read their anecdotes to each other.

○ Remind students to make eye contact as they tell the anecdote.

○ Have each group choose one member to share an anecdote with the whole class.

○ Ask the class, *Could this anecdote be used to make a point? What point could it make?* (Students are busy, The student's life is exciting, etc.)

After Listening

CRITICAL THINKING STRATEGY: Making Connections

○ Go over the information in the box.

○ Ask questions: *How does making connections help you? What are some things you can make connections to?*

TOEFL® iBT Tip

TOEFL iBT Tip 4: On the TOEFL iBT listening comprehension section, students will have to connect ideas that they've heard in a lecture with a reading topic.

○ Point out that the critical thinking strategy *Making Connections* will help students to understand relationships between ideas on different sections of the test and to synthesize information.

○ This will also be an important skill to use in integrated listening-reading-speaking and listening-reading-writing tasks.

EXPANSION ACTIVITY: Brainstorming Connections

○ Divide the class into small groups.

○ Write on the board the five different kinds of connections in the Critical Thinking Strategy box: *something you read, something you did, something you discussed, a class you took,* and *TV or radio.*

○ Have the students look back at the four ads on page 52 and brainstorm personal connections with the ads.

○ If possible, have students write one of each kind of connection for every ad.

○ Call on groups to share their answers with the class.

○ Ask: *Which kinds of connections were easy to make? Which were difficult?*

○ If you wish, you can make this activity competitive by giving the teams a point for every connection they think of. At the end of ten minutes, the team with the most points wins.

A. Making Connections

○ Go over the directions and the questions.

○ Put students in small groups to discuss the questions.

○ Call on students to share their ideas with the class.

ANSWER KEY

Answers will vary.

B. Extension
○ Go over the directions.
○ Have students design a T-shirt in pairs or small groups.
○ Have each group present their T-shirt design to the class.

PART ⑤ ACADEMIC ENGLISH
SELLING SNAPPLE IN JAPAN, PAGES 70–78

Before Listening
A. Thinking Ahead
○ Go over the directions.
○ Have students work in small groups to brainstorm ideas about drink types, ingredients, and words that describe the drinks. Remind students to write their ideas on the chart.
○ Call on students to share their ideas with the class.

ANSWER KEY
Answers will vary.

B. Vocabulary Preparation
○ Go over the directions.
○ Have students complete the sentences by writing the correct words on the lines.
○ Put students in pairs to compare answers.
○ Go over the answers with the class.

ANSWER KEY
1. fruit pulp; 2. seed; 3. nutritious; 4. thirst quenching;
5. highly desirable trait

TOEFL® iBT Tip

TOEFL iBT Tip 5: The TOEFL iBT will contain many vocabulary words that students may know in one context, but that they might not understand in a different context. For example, the vocabulary words in this activity (*seed, highly desirable trait*) could be applied to the field of biology or genetics as well as in a marketing context.

○ Point out that the *Vocabulary Preparation* activity will give students the opportunity to preview vocabulary words that will be heard in a lecture. This activity can be applied to many topics from the various fields that are presented on the TOEFL iBT.

○ Encourage students to do brainstorming activities on vocabulary chunks and phrases that might be used in marketing, biology, and other academic fields.

EXPANSION ACTIVITY: Original Sentences
○ Have students write original sentences using the vocabulary words.
○ Put students in pairs to compare sentences.
○ Call on students to read their sentences to the class.

C. Vocabulary Preparation: The Word *Market*
○ Go over the directions and the vocabulary words related to *market*.
○ Have students write the correct form of *market* in the reading.
○ Go over the answers with the class.

ANSWER KEY
1. market; 2. market/marketplace; 3. marketer;
4. market; 5. marketing

Academic Notes

○ Point out that students can expand their vocabulary more quickly if they learn word families, or groups of words that have the same base word. In Activity C on page 72, *market* is the base word, and the other words belong to the same word family.

○ You can generate a list of suffixes that are frequently used in word families.
Adjective endings: *–able, –ful, –less,*
Noun endings: *–er, –or, –ar, –ation, –ence/–ance*
Verbs: *–ate, –ize*
Adverbs: *–ly*

EXPANSION ACTIVITY: Word Families

○ Have students choose three new words from this chapter and write a list of words in their word families. Encourage students to use a dictionary to find words.

○ Have students compare word families with a partner.

D. Guessing the Meaning from Context

○ Go over the directions.

○ Have students read the sentences and write their guesses about the meaning of the words in red.

○ Have students compare ideas with a partner.

○ Call on students to share their ideas with the class.

ANSWER KEY

Answers will vary.
1. to make people like; 2. parts, sections; 3. products people buy and use quickly; 4. people coming and looking at products; 5. people who want to buy something; 6. advertisements that appear right in the store; 7. when people don't buy a product because it doesn't look good

Listening

A. Taking Notes: Using an Outline

○ Go over the directions.

○ Have students fill in the outline as you play the audio or video program. Repeat each section before continuing to the next.

Audio Script

Section 1

Lecturer: All right. Let's begin. Today's lecture is on a case study involving a marketing campaign initiated by the Quaker Oats Company [*points to board*] several years ago.

O.K. Now, in the United States, everyone knows the Quaker Oats Company for its good-tasting, high-quality food products. For many years, millions of cereal eaters have enjoyed its Quaker Oatmeal as a wholesome, nutritious breakfast food. And yet Quaker, which is noted for good marketing practices in the United States, experienced a major problem when it tried to introduce a new product into a foreign market.

What was the product? Snapple [*points to board*]. Snapple had been a popular beverage sold in the United States for several years. Now, the Snapple line of beverages included, um, a, uh, a wide assortment of iced tea and fruit-flavored drinks. Many of these drinks contained bits of fruit pulp and seeds of fruits such as strawberries and bananas used to make these drinks. And American customers liked the fresh, clean, thirst-quenching taste of these drinks. The fruit pulp and seeds at the bottom of the containers indicated that these drinks were made with fresh fruits, another highly desirable trait to American customers. The fruit pulp and seeds generated a *positive* attitude toward Snapple in the minds of American customers. As a result, this favorable attitude created an increasing demand for Snapple.

So, in January 1994, Quaker Oats introduced the line of Snapple iced tea and fruit-flavored beverages into Japan. These drinks, popular with many different segments of the U.S. beverage market, were not successful in Japan. Exactly three years later—in uh, January 1997—Quaker stopped shipping Snapple to Japan. Snapple, which was successfully marketed in the United States, failed after only three years in Japan. The question is: How could a major consumer-goods marketer like Quaker misunderstand the market so badly?

Section 2

Lecturer: When Quaker introduced Snapple in many Japanese retail stores, it used point-of-purchase displays [*points to board*]. Now, these displays featured attractive, attention-getting signs and a wide selection of Snapple drinks. These displays generated a large amount of customer traffic. Shoppers walking through stores went out of their way to visit the displays. However, while customer interest in Snapple was high, first-time sales were lower than anticipated. Repeat sales, that is, sales to customers that had already made an initial purchase of a Snapple drink, were also lower than anticipated.

It had soon become apparent that Snapple fruit drinks had an image problem with Japanese customers. Here's why: In 1994 most Japanese preferred clear beverages. In fact, in Japan, clarity denotes purity. The Japanese fruit drink customer feels that a clear fruit drink is both high quality and wholesome. Japanese consumers were quite interested in Snapple at first, walking up to the displays and, uh, examining the individual containers of Snapple. However, as customers examined the Snapple more closely, they noticed the fruit seeds and pulp at the bottom of the containers. This made them think that Snapple, while interesting, was not a high-quality, wholesome drink. And, if it was not a high-quality drink, why should they buy it?

When the Quaker Oats Company heard about this situation, the marketing people simply did not believe that the information correctly indicated Japanese customers' true feelings about Snapple. So, their response was something like this: "The seeds and pieces of fruit pulp indicate that real fruit was used to make the drinks, and is therefore a sign of quality. Strawberry and banana seeds are so small that no one can detect their presence in a fruit drink as it is consumed. In time, the Japanese customers will realize this. The sales of Snapple will continue to increase as more and more customers realize that Snapple, with its seeds and fruit pulp, is a high-quality drink." So uh, what was wrong with this thinking?

Section 3

Lecturer: Quaker may have made several important marketing mistakes when it introduced Snapple to Japan. Here are some ideas on what mistakes Quaker may have made. First, it seems as if little market research was done [points to board]. Quaker didn't try to understand the likes and dislikes of fruit juice customers in Japan. Now, market research is conducted before a product is introduced into a new market, to discover, uh, the potential new customers' likes and dislikes. Snapple was a successful product in the United States, but Japan was a new market for Snapple. Therefore, Quaker needed to treat Japan like any other market and conduct a thorough study of the

marketplace and its potential customers before it tried to sell Snapple in Japan.

Simple research into customer likes and dislikes would have shown that the Japanese had a strong dislike of fruit pulp and seeds in fruit drinks. So one mistake of Quaker was probably simply not knowing customers and what they like and dislike before introducing a new product into a new market. Now, this can be even more important when the new market is in another country. Frequently the customers in the potential new market have different attitudes, opinions, and beliefs. These must be identified and, uh, incorporated into the marketing planning before the new product is introduced.

Let's say Quaker management *knew* about the Japanese customers' preference for clear beverages. But it still decided to market Snapple with the fruit pulp and seeds anyway. If so, Quaker needed to develop a marketing campaign that addressed this problem. It needed to develop advertising and promotional efforts to change Japanese customers' perceptions about fruit and pulp from negative to positive. In other words, Quaker's advertisements could, uh, have said this: "Snapple fruit drinks contain fruit and seeds; but these really indicate quality and flavor."

Well, perhaps over time, Japanese customers would have changed their minds and, and have developed a liking for Snapple with its fresh fruit pulp and seeds. This way, Quaker would have a marketing advantage over other fruit drinks in Japan, which were clear. Snapple would have been the only drink with pulp and seeds. However, Quaker didn't use their advertising and promotional efforts to change customers' perceptions about the fruity pulp and seeds. So this probably was Quaker's second marketing mistake.

Section 4

Lecturer: A third potential mistake Quaker management made may have been due to the marketing of Snapple in the United States. Snapple was first sold along the East Coast in the United States. As it was sold in more and more parts of the U.S., uh, Snapple began to use up more and more of its management and financial resources [points to board]. Management and financial resources.

Management did not feel that they could afford either the time or the money to build production facilities to produce two lines of fruit drinks: one with fruit and seeds for sale in the U.S., and one without fruit and seeds for sale in Japan. Management felt that one type of drink, with fruit and seeds, could be successfully sold in two different markets. And so, it appears as if the Japanese market got the types of Snapple fruit juices that were most convenient for Snapple to manufacture, and not the types that were typically preferred in Japan.

Well, that wraps up the Snapple case study. Are there any questions before we move on?

ANSWER KEY

Selling Snapple in Japan

Section 1

I. Background

  A. The Quaker Oats Company

    1. Everyone knows it for its good tasting high-quality food products

    2. It recently had a problem with introducing a new product, Snapple, in Japan

  B. Snapple in the U.S.

    1. Snapple beverages included iced tea and fruit-flavored drinks

    2. Drinks contained pulp and seeds

  C. Failure in Japan after only three years

Section 2

II. Quaker Introduces Snapple in Japan

  A. Point-of-Purchase displays

    1. Looks: attractive, attention-getting

    2. Customer response: Interest was high; sales were low

  B. Product image problems

    1. In drinks, Japanese liked clarity, which indicates purity

    2. To the Japanese, Snapple was interesting, but not high-quality, wholesome

  C. Attitude of Quaker marketing department

    1. It didn't believe that the information indicated Japanese true feelings

    2. Sales will improve when Japanese realize that pulp means high-quality

Section 3

III. Quaker's 1st Marketing Mistake: Market Research

  A. Purpose of market research: to discover potential new customers' likes and dislikes

  B. Research would have shown that the Japanese had a strong dislike of fruit pulp and seeds in fruit drinks

  C. Research is important in another country because potential new customers may have different attitudes, opinions, and beliefs.

IV. Quaker's 2nd Marketing Mistake: Advertising

  A. Advertising could have changed customers perceptions about fruit pulp and fruit from negative to positive

  B. With advertising, Japanese customers might have changed their minds and developed a liking for Snapple

Section 4

V. Quaker's 3rd Marketing Mistake: Financial

  A. Quaker used up marketing and financial resources because it was being sold in more parts of the United States

  B. As a result, management could not produce two lines of fruit drinks (one for U.S. and one for Japan)

TOEFL® iBT Tip

TOEFL iBT Tip 6: Because The TOEFL iBT now allows note-taking, students need to learn the best strategies to take notes quickly and effectively from a lecture or from a written text.

○ Remind students that the activity for *Taking Notes* can help them to better organize their notes and facilitate finding information.

○ The ability to organize notes efficiently can also help learners make connections between the major and minor points in a lecture or conversation.

B. Checking Your Notes

○ Go over the directions.
○ Have students check their notes and fill in missing information as you play the audio or video program. Play all four sections without a break.
○ Put students in pairs to compare notes.
○ Go over the answers with the class.

ANSWER KEY

Use the outline for Activity A on page 42 of the Teacher's Edition.

LISTENING STRATEGY: Asking Questions

○ Go over the information in the box.
○ Ask comprehension questions: *Do all professors like students to ask questions during the lecture? If a professor likes questions at the end of the lecture, what should you do as you listen? Where and how should you write your questions? What are some things you might want to ask questions about?*

C. Asking Questions

○ Go over the directions.
○ Have students write three questions about the lecture.
○ Call on students to share their questions with the class.

ANSWER KEY

Answers will vary.

After Listening

A. Using Your Notes

○ Go over the directions and the questions.
○ Have students discuss the questions in pairs or small groups.
○ Call on students to share their answers with the class.

ANSWER KEY

1. the pulp and seeds; 2. colorful, attention-getting; 3. the pulp and seeds, because they liked clear drinks; 4. They didn't think the information they were getting gave the Japanese customers' true feelings; 5. They didn't do market research first, they didn't use advertising to change the Japanese perceptions, and they spent too much money on marketing and production in the United States so they didn't have the money to produce two lines of drinks.

B. Taking a Market Survey

○ Go over the directions.
○ Put students in groups. Have students survey the others in the group and write the responses on the chart. Remind students to put a check mark next to *Prefer* in the column of the drink they prefer.
○ Have each group compare answers with another group.
○ Call on students to report their findings to the class.

EXPANSION ACTIVITY: Online Ads

○ Photocopy and distribute the worksheet *Online Ads* on page BLM 5.
○ Have students read the information and answer the questions.
○ Go over the answers with the class.

ANSWER KEY

1. B; 2. C; 3. A; 4. B; 5. C

Put It All Together

A. Interviewing

○ Go over the directions. Have students read Steps 1 and 2 completely.
○ Have students choose a product and then answer the questions in Step 1.
○ Have students interview a classmate or someone else at the school. Remind students to describe the product and then ask the questions in Step 2.
○ Have students take notes on the interview.

B. Giving a Presentation

Step 1
○ Go over the directions and the steps.
○ Have students create an ad by drawing a picture and/or writing the copy.

SPEAKING STRATEGY: Outlining
○ Go over the information in the box.

Step 2
○ Have students complete the presentation outline.
○ Walk around the room to monitor the activity and provide help as needed.
○ Remind students to use what they learned in Activity A to create a presentation that will appeal to people at your school.

SPEAKING STRATEGY: Making Eye Contact
○ Go over the information in the box.
○ Ask comprehension questions: *How do you make eye contact? Why is this important when you make a presentation?*

EXPANSION ACTIVITY: Presentation Evaluation
○ Before students do Step 3 of Activity B, photocopy and distribute the worksheet *Feedback Form* on page BLM 4. Cut along the lines to separate the forms and give students enough copies to complete an evaluation of each member of their group.
○ Follow the procedure for Step 3 below.
○ Have students evaluate each presenter in the group.
○ After everyone in the group has presented, have students exchange evaluations.

Step 3
○ Put students in groups to take turns giving presentations. Remind students to make eye contact.
○ Explain that students will switch presenters every three minutes, until everyone in the group has presented.

Unit 1 Vocabulary Workshop

A. Matching
○ Go over the directions.
○ Have students write the correct letters on the lines
   to match the definitions with the words.
○ Go over the answers.

ANSWER KEY
1. b; 2. i; 3. d; 4. h; 5. c; 6. g 7. f; 8. j; 9. e; 10. a

B. True or False?
○ Go over the directions.
○ Have students fill in the correct bubbles.
○ Go over the answers.

ANSWER KEY
1. T; 2. F; 3. F; 4. F; 5. T; 6. T; 7. F; 8. F

C. High Frequency Words
○ Go over the directions.
○ Have students write the correct words on the lines.
○ Go over the answers.

ANSWER KEY
1. university; 2. first; 3. college; 4. second; 5. students;
6. four; 7. years; 8. four; 9. degree; 10. studies;
11. years; 12. receive; 13. years; 14. degree;
15. highest

UNIT 2 ●●●●● BIOLOGY

Unit Opener, page 81

○ Direct students' attention to the photo and the unit and chapter titles on page 81.
○ Brainstorm ideas about what the unit will include and write students' ideas on the board.

CHAPTER 3 ANIMAL BEHAVIOR

In Part 1, students will read three short stories about animal behavior. In Part 2, students will listen to students discuss animal emotions and intelligence. In Part 4, students will listen to a radio program about language learning and new research with two animals, a dog and an ape. In Part 5, students will listen to a lecture about the similarities and differences between humans and animals. Finally, students will research nonverbal communication in humans.

VOCABULARY

acquire	distinguish	inference	potential	species
adopt	dolphin	insult	predators	survive
aggressive	embarrassed	linguistic	prey	swept
body language	example	macaque	prodigy	syntax
border	facial expression	monkey	prompt	unconscious
branch	familiar	nonverbal communication	protect	wag
capacity	fetch	novel	remarkable	workaholic
colleague	grasp	on command	skeptic	you're kidding
crawl	hand gesture	otter	skeptical	zillion
detail	humans	point of view	slide	

LISTENING STRATEGIES

Understanding Emotion from Tone of Voice
Previewing: Thinking Before Listening
Knowing When to Take Notes
Including Details in Your Notes

CRITICAL THINKING STRATEGIES

Noticing Similarities (Part 1)
Making Inferences (Part 4)
Understanding a Speaker's Point of View (Part 5)
Note: Strategies in bold are highlighted in the Student Book.

MECHANICS OF LISTENING AND SPEAKING

Intonation: Changing Statements into Questions
Language Functions: Agreeing With Negative Questions
    Disagreeing With Negative Questions
Pronunciation: Reduced Forms of Words
Words in Phrases: Expressions of Disbelief and
    Skepticism

SPEAKING STRATEGY

Using Nonverbal Communication

TEST-TAKING STRATEGY

Listening for Stressed Words

CHAPTER 3 Animal Behavior

Chapter 3 Opener, page 83

○ Direct students' attention to the photo and chapter title. Go over the directions and questions.
○ Put students in pairs to discuss the questions.
○ Call on students to share their ideas with the class.

PART 1 INTRODUCTION
STRANGE BUT TRUE, PAGES 84–86

A. Thinking Ahead

○ Direct students' attention to the photos and ask questions: *What animals do you see? What are they doing?*
○ Go over the directions and the questions. Make sure students understand the words *predator, prey,* and *species.*
○ Put students in pairs to answer the questions.
○ Call on students to share their ideas with the class.

ANSWER KEY

Answers may vary.
1. Bulls, tortoises, and oryxes eat plants. Lions eat meat.
2. Lions are predators. Oryxes and tortoises are prey.
3. Answers will vary.

EXPANSION ACTIVITY: I Am Like a . . .

○ Model the activity. Tell students what kind of animal you are like. Explain that this is the animal you are most like now, not the one you would like to be (e.g., *I am like a tortoise because I am very shy and kind of slow*).
○ Have students choose an animal and then tell a partner which animal it is and how they are like it.
○ Call on students to tell the class about the animal.
○ In a variation, have students write the animal and three ways that they are like the animal.
○ Collect the descriptions. Read them aloud and have the class guess which student each animal represents.

B. Reading

○ Go over the directions and the questions.
○ Have students read the stories and think about the questions. They will answer the questions in Activity D.

Culture Notes

○ English has special phrases for groups of some kinds of animals. *A pride of lions* means a group of lions, but it would be incorrect to say a *pride of tigers* for a group of tigers. Other examples of such phrases are *a school of fish* and *a pod of whales.* Similar phrases for other species existed in old-fashioned English, but only a few are still commonly used.
○ Samburu National Park is about 220 miles north of Nairobi, Kenya.
○ Tsunamis are very large waves that are caused by earthquakes. In December of 2004, there was a terrible earthquake in the Indian Ocean, which triggered a huge tsunami.

Academic Note

○ Point out that rows of asterisks are sometimes used to separate sections of a story or different stories that have been grouped together. Extra line returns and number signs are also used in this way.

CRITICAL THINKING STRATEGY: Noticing Similarities

○ When an idea or image is repeated in different parts of a reading or lecture, it is probably important.
○ The reading in Activity B does not state a main idea. To understand the overall meaning, students must notice what is similar about the three different parts.

EXPANSION ACTIVITY: Strange Animal Stories

○ Have students use the Internet to search for "strange animal stories." Remind students that some websites are more reliable than others (i.e., .gov, .edu, news websites).
○ Put students in small groups to talk about one story they found on the Internet.
○ Call on students to share the story that they thought was the most strange. Ask the class if they think the story is really true.

C. Vocabulary Check
○ Go over the directions.
○ Have students write the words on the chart.
○ Put students in pairs to check their answers.
○ Go over the answers with the class.

ANSWER KEY
1. unconscious; 2. crawl; 3. protecting; 4. aggressive;
5. adopted; 6. swept; 7. survived

D. Discussion
○ Go over the directions and the questions.
○ Have students discuss the questions in small groups.
○ Call on students to share their ideas with the class.

ANSWER KEY
Answers may vary.
1. In each story, animals did something that was not expected, and they protected another kind of animal or a person.
2. Surprising actions: the cows protected the farmer from the bull, the lion adopted an oryx and protected it from other lions, and the hippo protected the tortoise from humans.
3. Answers will vary.

E. Journal Writing
○ Go over the directions.
○ Explain that this is a freewriting activity and does not have to be perfect. Point out that journal writing is a good warm-up for a more structured writing assignment, helping to generate ideas.
○ Set a time limit of five minutes.
○ Put students in pairs to read or talk about their writing.

TOEFL® iBT Tip

TOEFL iBT Tip 1: The TOEFL iBT requires examinees to synthesize information from spoken and written texts and respond in a speaking task or a writing task. Journal writing is a good way to help students express themselves openly in preparation for these types of tasks.

○ Point out that being able to read and explain or interpret a text will be helpful in building up to the integrated speaking task. The *Journal Writing* activity will help students to clearly articulate an opinion or describe a situation.

PART ② SOCIAL LANGUAGE
THAT DARN CAT, PAGES 87–93

Before Listening
A. Thinking Ahead
○ Go over the directions.
○ Direct students' attention to the photos.
○ Have students discuss the question in small groups.
○ Call on students to share their ideas with the class.

B. Taking a Survey
○ Go over the directions and the questions.
○ Direct students' attention to the chart and point out that the tally marks indicate the number of responses in each category.
○ Have students talk to 10 classmates, teachers, or students in other classes and record the answers in the chart.

EXPANSION ACTIVITY: Bar Graphs

○ Explain or review how to create bar graphs from data.
○ Draw a graph on the board (number of people on the vertical axis, responses on the horizontal axis as in the one below).

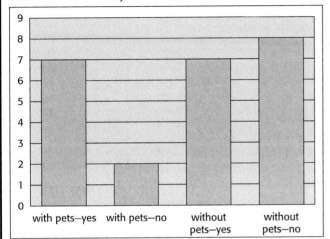

○ Ask a variation on the question in Activity B (*Do dogs feel emotions?*). Have students who say *yes* raise their hands. Tally the answers. Have students who say *no* raise their hands, and tally their answers. Put the results on the graph on the board.
○ Have students create their own bar graphs to show the results for Activity B. Remind students that they should have four bars: one for each response category (with pets – yes, with pets – no, without pets – yes, without pets – no).
○ Put students in pairs to compare graphs.

C. Discussing Survey Results

○ Go over the directions and the questions.
○ Have students discuss the questions in small groups.
○ Call on students to share ideas with the class.

ANSWER KEY

Answers will vary.

D. Brainstorming

○ Go over the directions and the questions.
○ Have students work in groups to brainstorm what they know about dolphins and answer the questions.
○ Call on students to share their ideas with the class.

Listening

🎧 A. Listening for the Main Idea

○ Go over the directions and the question.
○ Play the video or audio program.
○ Ask students: *What does each student believe about animals' emotions and intelligence?*

Audio Script

Brandon: Mmmm.
Tanya: Cream?
Brandon: Ah, no thanks.
Tanya: You coming down with something? Sounds like you got a cold.
Brandon: No, it's weird. It just started. I don't know what it is.
Jennifer: Well, I have a surprise. His name's Charlie.
Brandon and Tanya: Aw!
Tanya: Wait a minute. Is it gonna live here with us?
Jennifer: Not "it," *he.* Isn't he adorable?
Tanya: Yeah, he's adorable. Is he gonna live here with us?
Jennifer: Well, just for a few weeks, while Mr. Jensen's out of town. We're babysitting, uh, catsitting.
Tanya: Well, I'm not catsitting. You're catsitting.
Jennifer: O.K., O.K., O.K., I'll take care of him. But you'll like him. He's really smart. And he understands a lot.
Brandon: Yeah, you can tell. That cat's got a real intelligent face.
Tanya: Oh, come on.
Brandon: You see? I think you hurt his feelings. Don't listen to her.
Jennifer: Cats are very sensitive. You know, sometimes when a cat does something kind of stupid—I don't know, falls off a table or something—and everybody laughs? You can just tell that the cat feels really embarrassed. It hates to be laughed at.
Tanya: I don't buy that. Why do people always think that animals have the same emotions that humans have?
Jennifer: Because they do. And maybe they understand a lot more than we realize.
Brandon: Yeah, there are a zillion stories about how smart animals are.
Jennifer: Like dolphins. You know, sometimes they save a swimmer in the ocean who gets in trouble and can't swim back to the beach. They come right up, get right under the swimmer, and push him up to the surface. I don't understand it, but somehow they know.

CHAPTER 3 • Animal Behavior • 49

Brandon: Yeah, and elephants. Man, they're great animals.
Jennifer: And whales. I love whales.
Tanya: Well, it appears that one animal lover in this room is allergic to cats.
Brandon: You think?
Tanya: You mean you don't know?
Brandon: No. I've never had a cat. Maybe I am allergic.
Jennifer: I'm so sorry, Brandon. I didn't know.
Brandon: Me neither, obviously. Sorry, you guys. I got to get out of here. See you later.
Tanya: Bye.
Jennifer: Take care.

ANSWER KEY

Jennifer and Brandon believe that animals are intelligent and have emotions, but Tanya does not.

 B. Listening for Details

- ○ Go over the directions and the questions.
- ○ Have students answer the questions as you play the video or audio program a second time.
- ○ Put students in pairs to compare answers.
- ○ Go over the answers with the class.

Audio Script

Use the script for Activity A on page 49 of the Teacher's Edition.

ANSWER KEY

1. She is catsitting; 2. because they get embarrassed when they do something stupid and people laugh; 3. They save people who are drowning; 4. He is allergic to cats.

 TEST-TAKING STRATEGY: Listening for Stressed Words

- ○ Go over the information in the box and play the audio program.
- ○ Ask questions: *What words should you pay close attention to? Which words are stressed in the example sentences?*

C. Listening for Stressed Words

- ○ Go over the directions.
- ○ Have students write words from the box on the lines as you play the video or audio program.
- ○ Go over the answers with the class.

Audio Script

Jennifer: Cats are very sensitive. You know, sometimes when a cat does something kind of stupid—I don't know, falls off a table or something—and everybody laughs? You can just tell that the cat feels really embarrassed. It hates to be laughed at.
Tanya: I don't buy that. Why do people always think that animals have the same emotions that humans have?
Jennifer: Because they do. And maybe they understand a lot more than we realize.
Brandon: Yeah, there are a zillion stories about how smart animals are.
Jennifer: Like dolphins. You know, sometimes they save a swimmer in the ocean who gets in trouble and can't swim back to the beach. They come right up, get right under the swimmer, and push him up to the surface.

ANSWER KEY

1. sensitive; 2. stupid; 3. laughs; 4. embarrassed; 5. hates; 6. animals; 7. humans; 8. do; 9. zillion; 10. smart; 11. dolphins; 12. trouble; 13. beach; 14. push

LISTENING STRATEGY: Understanding Emotion from Tone of Voice

- ○ Go over the information in the box and play the audio program.
- ○ Ask questions: *What is intonation? Why is it important to pay attention to intonation?*

TOEFL iBT Tip 2: The TOEFL iBT listening and speaking sections will test the examinee's abilities to understand the attitude, purpose or motivation, or degree of certainty of the speaker.

○ Point out that the activity *Understanding Emotion from Tone of Voice* will help students to understand a speaker's general opinion about a topic.

○ Mention that the stress and intonation of the speaker will help students interpret the speaker's intended meaning.

D. Understanding Emotion from Tone of Voice

○ Go over the directions.
○ Have students fill in the correct bubbles as you play the audio program.
○ Have students check their answers in pairs.
○ Go over the answers with the class.

Audio Script

1. **A:** I'm going out of town. Could you take care of my cat for a few days?
   B: O.K. [*agrees and is excited*]
2. **A:** This is the *fourth* cat you've brought home. We *can't* have any more animals.
   B: O.K., O.K., O.K. [*agrees unhappily*]
3. **A:** My cat can obey commands. When I say sit, she sits.
   B: You're kidding. [*is surprised, but believes A*]
4. **A:** Phil's parrot can talk. It can answer questions.
   B: You're kidding. [*doesn't believe A*]

ANSWER KEY
1. A; 2. B; 3. A; 4. B

After Listening
A. Check Your Understanding
○ Go over the directions.
○ Put students in pairs to discuss the question.
○ Call on students to share their ideas with the class.

ANSWER KEY
Jennifer and Brandon think that animals are intelligent and have emotions, but Tanya doesn't agree.

B. Vocabulary Check: Words for Emotions
○ Direct students' attention to the chart on page 91 and the photos on page 92.
○ Go over the directions.
○ Have students fill in the noun or adjective form of each word in the chart.
○ Have students write an adjective under each picture on page 92 and then compare answers with a partner.
○ Call on students to share their answers with the class.

ANSWER KEY

Nouns	Adjectives
1. amazement	amazed
2. anger	angry
3. confusion	confused
4. embarrassment	embarrassed
5. fear	fearful/afraid
6. happiness	happy
7. pride	proud
8. sadness	sad
9. satisfaction	satisfied
10. skepticism	skeptical

Answers for A–I may vary.
A. confused; B. proud; C. amazed; D. satisfied; E. angry; F. fearful/afraid; G. skeptical; H. embarrassed; I. sad

C. Interviewing
○ Go over the directions.
○ Have students interview three classmates and record the answers on the chart.
○ Call on students to tell the class what they found out.

ANSWER KEY
Answers will vary.

EXPANSION ACTIVITY: Emotions
○ Brainstorm sentences that students might say in the course of a day (e.g., *Do you want to get some coffee? I can't understand this assignment.*) and write them on the board.
○ Call volunteers to the board. Point to a sentence and whisper an emotion (e.g., *embarrassed, angry, excited, sad, confused*).
○ Have the student say the sentence in the right tone of voice. Elicit the emotion from the class.
○ Repeat the activity until everyone has had a chance to participate or until students have guessed all the emotions correctly.

PART ③ THE MECHANICS OF LISTENING AND SPEAKING, PAGES 93–97

INTONATION: Changing Statements into Questions
○ Go over the information in the box. Play the audio program.
○ Ask comprehension questions: *How is the intonation different when you change a statement to a question? What does the rising intonation show?*

A. Intonation in Statements and Questions
○ Go over the directions.
○ Have students check the correct answer as you play the audio program.

○ Repeat if necessary.
○ Go over the answers with the class.

Audio Script
1. He has a cat?
2. She doesn't believe you.
3. He went to Bermuda?
4. This isn't your cat?
5. I'm allergic to cats.
6. He went to Bermuda.
7. You've gone swimming with dolphins?
8. She doesn't believe you?

ANSWER KEY
1. question; 2. statement; 3. question; 4. question; 5. statement; 6. statement; 7. question; 8. question

EXPANSION ACTIVITY: Pair Work
○ Have students write four statements.
○ Put students in pairs to practice saying each sentence as a statement and as a question.
○ In a variation, have students dictate their sentences to a partner and then check for correct ending punctuation (*. or ?*).

LANGUAGE FUNCTIONS: Agreeing With Negative Questions
○ Go over the information in the box.
○ Ask comprehension questions: *How do you respond to a negative question in English if you want to agree? What else do we often do when we answer a negative question?*

B. Agreeing With Negative Questions
○ Go over the directions and the roles of Students A and B.
○ Have students take turns asking and answering negative questions in pairs.
○ Walk around the room to monitor the activity and provide help as needed.
○ Call on students and ask negative questions, eliciting agreement.

🎧 Disagreeing With Negative Questions

○ Go over the information in the box. Play the audio program.
○ Ask questions: *How do we disagree with a negative question in English? How can you make the meaning of your answer clear?*

C. Disagreeing With Negative Questions

○ Go over the directions.
○ Have students take turns asking and answering negative questions in pairs.
○ Walk around the room to monitor the activity and provide help as needed.
○ Call on students and ask negative questions, eliciting disagreement.

D. Negative Questions

○ Go over the directions and the examples.
○ Have students write three negative questions each about the conversation in Part 2.
○ Put students in groups of three to take turns asking and answering negative questions with the correct information.

Grammar Notes

○ Explain that negative questions can be asked either with or without a tag question.
○ In a tag question, the helping verb and subject are repeated at the end of a statement. For example, the negative question *You don't like coffee?* can also be said as *You don't like coffee, do you?*
○ When the main verb in a statement is negative, the verb in the tag question is positive. When the main verb is positive, the verb in the tag question is negative.

EXPANSION ACTIVITY: Tag Questions

○ Have students rewrite each of Student A and Student B's negative questions in Activity B with a tag question.
○ Call on students and have them ask one of the questions with and without a tag. Give feedback on correct grammar and intonation.

🎧 PRONUNCIATION: Reduced Forms of Words

○ Go over the information in the box. Play the audio program.
○ Ask comprehension questions: *What is the short form of* don't know? *What is the long form of* gotta?

🎧 E. Reduced Forms of Words

○ Go over the directions.
○ Have students write the long forms of the words they hear as you play the audio program.
○ Put students in pairs to compare answers.
○ Go over the answers with the class.

Audio Script

A: Are you gonna take Biology 121 next term?
B: I might. Is Dr. Hurst teaching it?
A: Yeah, I think so. You'll like 'er.
B: Well, Brandon says she's really hard.
A: Oh, don't listen to 'im. Besides, you know, you gotta take it before you take Biology 152. And it's a required class. You can't get outta taking it some time.

ANSWER KEY

1. going to; 2. her; 3. him; 4. got to; 5. out of

WORDS IN PHRASES: Expressions of Disbelief and Skepticism

○ Go over the information in the box. Play the audio program.
○ Ask comprehension questions: *What are some ways to express disbelief? Can you use these expressions in any situation?*

TOEFL iBT Tip 3: The TOEFL iBT tests the ability to listen for a speaker's purpose or motivation, attitude, or degree of certainty in conversations or lectures.

❍ Point out that the mechanics box *Expressions of Disbelief and Skepticism* will help students to understand some of the phrases that native speakers of English use to convey meaning in conversation.

❍ Remind students that some expressions are not literal and have to be learned as idioms.

Put It Together

Step 1
❍ Go over the directions and examples.
❍ Have students write seven negative sentences that they think are true.

Step 2
❍ Go over the directions.
❍ Model the activity. Call on a student to read one of his or her sentences as a question. Respond by agreeing or disagreeing appropriately. Switch roles. Express disbelief.
❍ Have students take turns in pairs reading the sentences as questions and responding appropriately.
❍ Walk around to monitor the activity and provide help as needed.

PART BROADCAST ENGLISH THE EDUCATION OF RICO AND KANZI, PAGES 98–102

Before Listening

A. Thinking Ahead
❍ Direct students' attention to the photos and ask questions: *Which animal do you think is smarter? Which one will obey people better?*
❍ Go over the directions.

❍ Have students check their answers to the questions in the chart.
❍ Have students discuss the questions in pairs or small groups.
❍ Call on students to share their ideas with the class.

ANSWER KEY
Answers will vary.

EXPANSION ACTIVITY: Vote with Your Feet
❍ Write *Agree* on one side of the board and *Disagree* on the other.
❍ Explain that you will say a sentence and students should stand near the word that expresses their opinion.
❍ Call a group of students to the board. Say: *Animals can use tools like humans do.* Remind students to stand near *Agree* or *Disagree*.
❍ Ask students to explain their position. Tell students that the next two listening segments will address some of these ideas.
❍ Say other sentences. Use your own or the ones below. You may want to have different groups of students come to the board.
Animals can create sentences.
Most animals like to play.
Animals can express embarrassment, fear, and anger.
Although parrots can imitate speech, they don't really know what they are saying.

B. Vocabulary Preparation
❍ Go over the directions.
❍ Have students write the words or phrases on the lines.
❍ Put students in pairs to compare answers.
❍ Go over the answers with the class.

ANSWER KEY
1. prompt; 2. linguistic; 3. remarkable/prodigies; 4. acquired; 5. border; 6. familiar; 7. skeptics; 8. colleagues; 9. workaholic

EXPANSION ACTIVITY: Beanbag Toss

○ Tell students they have one minute to review the vocabulary from Activity B.

○ After one minute, ask students to close their books.

○ Tell students that you will call on a student and toss a ball or beanbag. You will say one of the definitions, and the students should respond with the vocabulary word or phrase and throw the beanbag back.

○ Call on a student and toss the beanbag, saying *amazing.* Elicit an answer from the student (*remarkable*) and have them toss the beanbag or ball back to you.

○ Repeat with other students. This is a fast-paced activity.

Listening

🎧 **A. Listening for the Main Idea: Section 1**

○ Go over the directions.

○ Have students listen for the answers to the questions as you play the audio program.

○ Go over the answers with the class.

Audio Script

Siegel: If you think your dog understands you and is getting better at it, scientists say you may be right. New research shows not only can dogs understand human speech, they can learn new words the same way children do. The finding is published in this week's issue of the journal *Science*. NPR's Jon Hamilton has the story.

Hamilton: Every species has its prodigies. In the dog world, one of these is a Border collie in Germany named Rico. He knows literally hundreds of words. Julia Fischer is a senior researcher at the Max Planck Institute for Evolutionary Anthropology in Leipzig. She and her colleagues learned about Rico several years ago while watching TV.

Fischer: There's a German program called *Wetten, Dass...?*; that's something like "I betcha." And this is a show where people—everyday people can say, "I can do amazing things. You know, I can tell the color of my crayons from just, you know, sucking on them."

Hamilton: Rico did something a little more interesting from a scientific point of view. He showed he could fetch any one of his 70 toys on command. Since then, Rico has acquired a lot more toys and added nearly 200 words to his vocabulary. Fischer and her colleagues have lots of videotapes of Rico working with his owner.

Unidentified Woman: Rico, [*German spoken*]

Hamilton: Skeptics out there should know that Rico isn't being prompted in any way.

Unidentified Woman: [*German spoken*]

Hamilton: What Fischer's team really wanted to know was whether Rico could learn new words the way children do. Fischer says if any dog could make the leap, it would be Rico.

Fischer: He's a workaholic. He's crazy. I mean, he just goes on and on and on and on, and the owner has to stop him. She has to go—she sees when he gets tired, so—you know, he has red eyes then. And he forgets to drink and eat. I mean, I've never seen that before in a dog.

Hamilton: So the scientists put seven of Rico's familiar toys and one new toy in a room. They asked Rico to fetch the new toy using a word for it that he'd never heard before. Rico brought back the right toy. More important, he often added its name to his vocabulary. A month later, Rico was able to remember a new toy's name about half the time even though he'd heard the word only once. Sue Savage-Rumbaugh is a biology professor at Georgia State University. She says that's a remarkable achievement.

Savage-Rumbaugh: We know now that the dog can rapidly associate new words with new objects, which is what children do right at the point that language takes off, becomes very complex, grammar production pops in. So the dog's on the borderline of very complex language ability.

ANSWER KEY

New research shows us that dogs can learn words the same way children do. Rico knows hundreds of words and can fetch toys on command.

🎧 B. Listening for Details

○ Go over the directions.
○ Have students write the answers on the lines as you play the audio program.
○ Go over the answers with the class.

Audio Script

Use the script for Activity A on page 55 of the Teacher's Edition.

ANSWER KEY

1. hundreds of words; 2. 70; 3. 200; 4. He fetched the right toy; 5. Answers will vary.

🎧 C. Listening for the Main Idea: Section 2

○ Go over the directions.
○ Have students answer the question as you play the audio program.
○ Go over the answer with the class.

Audio Script

Hamilton: Savage-Rumbaugh is also working on dog vocabulary these days, but she's best known for her work with apes that appear to have crossed that linguistic border. Her prize pupil is a bonobo named Kanzi, who, like Rico, has appeared in lots of videotapes.
Savage-Rumbaugh: Kanzi, can you put the pine needles in the refrigerator? Good job. Thank you.
Hamilton: Savage-Rumbaugh says Kanzi has provided the most convincing evidence yet that animals can learn not only words, but grammar.
Savage-Rumbaugh: Kanzi understands syntax; he understands novel sentences when he's heard them for the first time. Kanzi can overhear conversations in the other room and even report about what he's heard.

Hamilton: Such abilities challenge the theory that only modern humans have the capacity for language. Stuart Shanker of York University in Toronto is a co-author of an upcoming book called *The First Idea* about the ideas of the origins of symbols, language, and intelligence. Shanker says many species appear to have the potential to communicate with humans. Whether they actually do, he says, depends less on a specialized brain than on the sort of interactions that they have with people.
Siegel: You can see video of Rico learning a new word—and there's more about animal communication—at our website, npr.org.

ANSWER KEY

Animals can learn not only words, but grammar.

🎧 D. Listening for Details

○ Go over the directions.
○ Have students answer the questions as you play the audio program.
○ Have students compare answers with a partner.
○ Go over the answers with the class.

Audio Script

Use the script for Activity C above.

ANSWER KEY

1. Answers will vary, but Kanzi should be in a box to the right of Rico's box, because his linguistic ability is more complex.
2. Rico can understand grammar, understand novel sentences, overhear conversations in the next room, and report about what he's heard.

CRITICAL THINKING STRATEGY: Making Inferences

○ Go over the information in the box.
○ Ask questions: *What does it mean to make inferences? Why is it important to make inferences?*

TOEFL® iBT Tip

TOEFL iBT Tip 4: The TOEFL iBT tests the examinee's ability to make inferences based on information presented in a conversation or lecture.

○ Point out that the critical thinking strategy *Making Inferences* will help students to determine what an author means when information is not stated directly in a lecture.

○ By using key words and phrases from the lecture (and through organized note-taking), students will be able to apply this skill to the listening comprehension section of the test. This skill will also be very important when synthesizing information in the integrated tasks on the test.

E. Making Inferences

○ Go over the directions.
○ Have students answer the questions as you play the audio program.
○ Go over the answers with the class.

Audio Script

Hamilton: Savage-Rumbaugh is also working on dog vocabulary these days, but she's best known for her work with apes that appear to have crossed that linguistic border. Her prize pupil is a bonobo named Kanzi, who, like Rico, has appeared in lots of videotapes.
Savage-Rumbaugh: Kanzi, can you put the pine needles in the refrigerator? Good job. Thank you.

ANSWER KEY
1. an ape; 2. yes, because the woman said "Good job."

After Listening

A. Discussion

○ Go over the directions and the questions.
○ Put students in small groups to discuss the questions.
○ Call on students to share their ideas with the class.

ANSWER KEY
Answers will vary.

EXPANSION ACTIVITY: Debate

○ Divide the class into small groups and assign each group one of the following animals: dog, cat, dolphin, parrot, horse, whale. You don't need to use all the animals if you have fewer than six groups.
○ Have the students discuss the animals in their groups and write reasons why their group's animal is the smartest animal on the list. Set a time limit of 10 minutes. Explain that they will try to persuade their classmates that their animal is the smartest.
○ Call on group members and have them present reasons why their group's animal is the smartest.
○ If you wish, have the class vote on the smartest animal.

B. Extension

○ Go over the directions and the steps. For a variation on the presentation, see the activity that follows.
○ Have students do research on the Internet and take notes on one animal in the chart.
○ Put students in pairs or small groups to share what they learned. You may want to group students so that each animal is represented in the small group. Have group members take notes on the other animals.
○ Call on students to share their ideas with the class.

VARIATION ACTIVITY: Expert Groups and Home Groups

○ Put students in groups of four (Home Groups). Assign each student in a group one of the four animals in the chart.
○ Have students research the animal.
○ Have students compare their findings with other students who researched the same animal (Expert Groups).
○ Put students back in their original group of four (Home Groups).
○ Have students report their findings to the group as the others take notes in the chart.

ANSWER KEY

Answers may vary.

Animal	Species	Scientist(s)	What this Animal Can Do or Has Learned
Kanzi	bonobo	Sue Savage-Rumbaugh	Can use over 200 words productively (through a keyboard), over 500 words receptively Can listen through headphones and identify the word Can use and make tools
Alex	parrot	Irene Pepperburg	Knows 100 words Can identify 50 different objects and recognize quantities up to six Can distinguish seven colors and five shapes Can understand "bigger," "smaller," "same" and "different" Is learning the concepts of "over" and "under"
Washoe	chimpanzee	Beatrix and Allan Gardner, Roger Fouts	Knows American Sign Language (200 signs) Can make up words
Koko	gorilla	Dr. Francine "Penny" Patterson	Knows 1000 words in ASL Has invented words and Gorilla Sign Language Expresses emotions

PART ⑤ ACADEMIC ENGLISH
HUMANS AND OTHER ANIMALS, PAGES 103–109

Before Listening

LISTENING STRATEGY: Previewing: Thinking Before Listening

○ Go over the information in the box.
○ Ask questions: *How can you be a more active listener? What was surprising in the lecture in Chapter 1?*

A. Previewing: Thinking Before Listening

○ Go over the directions and the questions. Make sure students understand the words in bold: *insulted, distinguishes, otter, monkey.*
○ Put students in pairs to discuss the questions.
○ Call on students to share their ideas with the class.

ANSWER KEY

Answers will vary.

SPEAKING STRATEGY: Using Nonverbal Communication

○ Go over the information in the box.
○ Ask questions: *What is* body language? *What is an example of a* hand gesture?
○ Have students turn to page 92. Elicit ideas about what each person in the photos is communicating.

B. Using Nonverbal Communication

○ Go over the directions.
○ Model the activity. Use nonverbal communication to convey one of the ideas in the box. Elicit the idea from the class.
○ Have students take turns in pairs nonverbally communicating the ideas in the box and guessing.
○ Call on students to communicate an idea and elicit the idea from the class.

Culture Note

○ Remind students that some types of nonverbal communication are the same throughout the world, while others are specific to cultures. The expansion activity that follows will help students identify some of these cultural differences.

EXPANSION ACTIVITY: Describing Nonverbal Communication

○ Put students in small groups to brainstorm and write down different nonverbal ways of expressing the emotions in the box on page 92. If possible, have students from different cultures work together.
○ Call on groups to describe the nonverbal communication they thought of. Note which group thought of the most ways to express each emotion.
○ Write a complete list on the board of the different ways to express each emotion. Ask students if any of the nonverbal communication is unfamiliar to them. Point out any cultural differences.

LISTENING STRATEGY: Knowing When to Take Notes

○ Go over the information in the box.
○ Ask questions: *Why is it important to take good notes during lectures? What are some signals the professor uses that can let you know you should take notes?*

C. Knowing When to Take Notes

○ Go over the directions.
○ Direct students' attention to the chart on page 105.
○ Ask students the questions and elicit answers.

ANSWER KEY

Information to write down: what humans and non-human animals do in four areas
Words: wag, slide, galah, grasp, branch; macaque

Listening

A. Taking Notes

○ Go over the directions and the questions.
○ Point out that students will have to guess the meaning of some vocabulary from the lecturer's body language or the general context.
○ Have students fill in the chart as you play the video or audio program.
○ Remind students to write not only what the lecturer writes in the chart, but also other important details from the lecture. Explain that the students' charts do not have to look exactly the same as the one the lecturer makes.
○ Go over the answers with the class. You may want to reproduce the chart on the board and have volunteers fill it in.

Audio Script

Section 1

Lecturer: Good morning, everyone. I hope you all had a good weekend. Before we get started today can everyone please make sure their cell phones are turned off. O.K. Thank you very much. I appreciate that. Thanks. O.K. Over the weekend, besides the reading, I sincerely hope you considered the question that I'll be exploring today: What distinguishes humans from other animals? Oh, and please don't feel insulted that I am calling humans "animals," right? You understand that I am speaking biologically, yes? O.K. Good.

So. Our question for the day. Humans and non-humans. [*writes on board*] As you'll see, the answer has been changing, thanks to recent research and discoveries.

Today, we're going to cover only four areas: emotion, [*writes on board*] that's one, tool use, [*writes on board*] learning, [*writes on board*] and language. [*writes on board*]

First, emotion . . . love, hate, anger, embarrassment, fear, even a sense of *fun.* Of course, humans experience emotion every day. Do we all agree? O.K., how about animals? What do you think? How many of you have pets? Well, most of us who have been around domestic dogs, cats, horses, and even birds think that these animals *also* have emotions, or at least *appear* to have emotions. Uh, for example, when a dog wags its tail, [*moves hand back and forth*] it's clear to us that the dog is happy, or enthusiastic. Similarly, it seems clear that dogs can express sadness, along with other emotions.

Many animals in the wild also seem to express emotion, such as enjoyment, fun. For example, otters sometimes slide down a small hill into the water, [*slides hand down*] swim back to the beach, [*makes swimming motion*] climb up the hill, [*raises arms over head*] and slide down again, [*slides hand down*] over and over. This appears to be for no other reason than *fun.* It's play behavior. Another very cute example of play behavior is in Australia, where parrots called "galahs" will fly to the top of a building that holds corn or grain. They grasp [*closes hand*] a support wire with their feet, then slide down to the ground [*slides hand down*]. Now, they do this over and over. There's a beauty in this play behavior, and it is easy to see that the animals enjoy it.

So it seems obvious to many people that animals do have emotions. But the problem is *proving* it, scientifically. Modern researchers who scientifically study emotions in humans believe that humans have emotions because they can *say* with *words* that they do have emotions. But, because other animals can't speak in *words,* researchers aren't sure that they have emotions.

There is, however, a possible solution. For both humans and non-humans, scientists can watch their *nonverbal body language* such as facial expressions and hand gestures. The scientists record different *sounds* that often seem to go *with* emotion—sounds that are not words, such as screams of anger. There have been many studies like this on humans. Now, when scientists do this type of study with other animals, they see the fact that the nonverbal language of humans is very similar to the nonverbal language of many other animals. However, there haven't yet been many studies on this.

Section 2

Lecturer: Now, how 'bout tool use? [*points to board*] Of course, humans use tools. [*writes on board*] But other animals? Well, for many years, until fairly recently, the answer was "no." Scientists always used to say that one characteristic that distinguishes humans from other animals is tool use. In other words, only humans use tools. But then in the 1960s, a young researcher named Jane Goodall [*writes on board*] was observing wild chimps [*writes on board*] in a place called Gombe, in Tanzania, Africa. She made an amazing discovery. The chimps in that area take a thin branch from a tree or bush and use it to stick into a small hill where termites live. Why? These insects are important food for chimps. Good protein. But they're impossible to reach in their hills. But when the chimps pull the branch out, there are hundreds of termites on the branch. Dinner! So why did I call this discovery "amazing"? Because for the first time, a researcher saw the use of a *tool* by a non-human, in the wild, in nature. [*writes on board*] There have been many other such discoveries since then, but this was the first.

Section 3

Lecturer: O.K. On to learning [*writes on board*]. Humans learn all the time, right? Okay, yeah, some learn more than others. But what about other animals? Scientists used to believe that only humans learn. This makes us different from other animals. But then . . . there was another amazing discovery on a beach in Japan. For a long time, scientists studied a group of macaques there. [*writes on board*] This is a kind of monkey. Anyway, the scientists watched these guys for a long time. They watched, for example, as every day the macaques ate sweet potatoes. But then, one day— and nobody will ever know why—one young female took her sweet potato down to the water and *washed off the sand before she ate it.* This had never happened before. And even more amazing . . . you know what happened after that? Her mother started washing her sweet potatoes. Then other young females washed theirs. Now this *whole group of macaques* is famous for washing their food. No other group does it. So what does this prove? Yes. *Learning.* [*writes on board*] Okay. One more example of learning in the wild (I mean, not a zoo, right?). Remember those chimps in Tanzania? They *learn* how to use that tool to get termites. They *learn by watching their mothers.*

Section 4

Lecturer: One more area. Language. Humans have it [*writes on board*]. But other animals? They make sounds, of course, and some of these sounds have meaning. But can they learn to understand and use *language*—not just *sounds*? Well . . . there have been a number of studies in recent years, with different kinds of animals. Oh, this reminds me . . . did any of you happen to hear that radio program about that dog in Germany, Rico? Great. Well, you noticed that this dog is able to understand a lot of words and also understands some *syntax*—the order of words and how this order changes the meaning. But of course Rico doesn't *produce* language.

There are many other studies going on now, some with chimps, some with gorillas, some with parrots—talking birds. Uh, the chimps and gorillas aren't able to actually speak, of course, because of their vocal tract [*indicates throat*], so in these studies, they learn sign language, [*shows hand*] you know, gestures with their hands—or a special computer language with symbols. Anyway, for homework, you're going to read about these studies, and we'll discuss them next time, but just to give you an idea about this . . . the research questions are, "Can non-human animals create new words, and can they put words together into new, um, *original* sentences?" What do you think? Well, the answer is . . . to a certain degree, yes. There's a gorilla named Koko [*writes on board*] for example, who didn't know the word *ring*, [*points to finger*] so . . . she created the term "finger bracelet" [*indicates wrist*] instead. Pretty good, huh? Anyone could understand that, even though the term doesn't exist. Another example. There's a parrot named Alex [*writes on board*] who didn't know the word *apple* and so created a new word for it—*banerry*—a combination of *banana* and *cherry*—two words for fruit that he *did* know. One last example. There's a chimp named Kanzi [*writes on board*] who is able to create simple sentences such as "You, me, go out, hurry." So can we say that other animals can learn language? Yes. It's limited, but it's there [*writes on board*].

O.K. So what can we conclude from this ? Well, um, we can't say much yet about emotion. [*writes on board*] But the other areas . . . humans and other animals are beginning to look pretty similar, huh? So what's the difference? Well, some animals can use simple tools but they can't build an airplane. Animals can learn, but they can't learn higher mathematics. Animals can learn some language, but "You, me, go out, hurry" is not exactly Shakespeare. So what can we conclude? In these four areas, humans and other animals have many of the same abilities. We are very similar. The difference? Humans do all of this [*Indicates board*] *more*. The difference is only of *degree*. We do it all more.

O.K. That's it for today. You know the chapters to read tonight, right?

ANSWER KEY

Areas	Humans	Non-humans
1. emotion	yes	Dogs—wag tails Otters—slide down hills Galahs—slide down wire
2. tool use	Yes	Chimps—use branch to get termites to eat (Jane Goodall, Tanzania)
3. learning	yes	Macaques—learn to wash sweet potatoes (Japan) Chimps—learn to use tool to get termites (Tanzania)
4. language	Yes	Rico (dog)—understands words and syntax Koko (gorilla)—created sign language for ring Alex (parrot)—created word for apple (banerry) Kanzi (chimp)—created simple sentences (you, me, go out, hurry)

Vocabulary
wag: wave back and forth
slide: move smoothly across a surface
galah: parrot
grasp: hold
branch: part of tree or bush
macaque: a kind of monkey

Note: Because the definitions of *wag*, *slide*, and *grasp* must be guessed from the lecturer's body language, answers for these items will vary.

LISTENING STRATEGY: Including Details in Your Notes

○ Go over the information in the box.
○ Ask questions: *When will you find out if your notes are good? What is one kind of detail you should take notes about? What words often introduce examples?*

TOEFL® iBT Tip

TOEFL iBT Tip 5: Because the TOEFL iBT now allows note-taking, students need to learn the best strategies to take notes quickly and effectively.

○ Remind students that the listening strategy *Including Details in Your Notes* can help them to distinguish between the major points and important details of a lecture or a conversation.

○ Listening for signals such as *for example* or *such as* helps students to notice important details that may later be tested.

B. Checking Your Notes for Details

○ Go over the directions.
○ Have students see if they can answer the questions in After Listening Activities A, B, and C.
○ Have students check and complete their notes as you play the video or audio program again.
○ Put students in pairs to compare their notes.
○ Go over the answers with the class.

Audio Script

Use the script for Activity A on page 59 of the Teacher's Edition.

ANSWER KEY

Use the chart for Activity A on page 61 of the Teacher's Edition.

After Listening

A. Using Your Notes: Checking Main Ideas

○ Go over the directions and the questions.
○ Have students discuss the questions in small groups.
○ Call on students to share their answers with the class.

ANSWER KEY

Ways they are similar: Both can show emotions nonverbally, use tools, learn, and use language. Ways they are different: Humans can show emotions with words, use many tools, learn much more, and use complex language. Humans "do it all more."

B. Using Your Notes: Checking Details

○ Go over the directions.
○ Have students answer the questions and then compare answers with a partner.
○ Go over the answers with the class.

ANSWER KEY

1. dogs, otters, galahs; 2. happiness, enthusiasm, enjoyment, fun; 3. dog wags tail, otters slide and swim, galahs slide; 4. chimps using branches; 5. sticks it in a termite hole to get termites; 6. Jane Goodall; 7. Gombe in Tanzania, Africa; 8. macaques learned to wash sweet potatoes and chimps learned to use tool to get termites; 9. macaques learned to wash sweet potatoes and chimps learned to use tool for termites; 10. in Japan and in Africa; 11. Koko—gorilla, Alex—parrot, Kanzi—chimp; 12. Koko—*finger bracelet* (for *ring*), Alex—*banerry* (for *apple*), Kanzi—*You, me, go out, hurry*

C. Using Your Notes: Checking Vocabulary

○ Go over the directions.
○ Have students work with a partner to discuss the words.
○ Call on students to share their ideas with the class.

ANSWER KEY

1. wag: (wave hands back and forth), slide (use hand in swooshing motion, starting high and ending low), grasp (use hand to grab), branch (hold out arms like the branches of a tree)
2. A galah is a kind of bird; A macaque is a kind of monkey.

CRITICAL THINKING STRATEGY:
Understanding a Speaker's Point of View
○ Go over the information in the box.
○ Ask comprehension questions: *What does* point of view *mean? Does a speaker always state his or her opinion directly? How can you infer a point of view?*

TOEFL® iBT Tip

TOEFL iBT Tip 6: The TOEFL iBT tests the ability to understand a speaker's point of view and the speaker's motivation for making a statement.

○ The critical thinking strategy *Understanding a Speaker's Point of View* will help students to make inferences or form generalizations based on what a speaker has implied.

○ This strategy will be useful in the integrated tasks of the TOEFL iBT, where examinees are required to listen to a lecture, read a text, and then respond orally or in writing.

D. Understanding a Speaker's Point of View
○ Go over the directions.
○ Have students answer the questions.
○ Call on students to share their answers with the class.

ANSWER KEY
1. Yes, he calls the behavior *play behavior.* 2. Yes, he thinks the example is very cute.

E. Making Connections
○ Go over the directions.
○ Have students discuss the questions in pairs.
○ Call on students to share their ideas with the class.

ANSWER KEY
Answers may vary.
1. Animals are intelligent enough to learn and can express some emotions.
2. Answers will vary.

Put It All Together
A. Doing Research
○ Go over the directions.
○ Have the students read the steps.
Step 1
○ Have students choose one situation.
○ Discuss where students can find the subjects they chose to observe.
Step 2
○ Go over the directions and the example.
○ Remind students to watch the situation and record their observations in the chart before the next class.
Step 3
○ Go over the directions and the example.
○ Remind students that if they are uncertain what a piece of nonverbal communication means, they can guess.

B. Reporting Results
○ Go over the directions.
○ Have students discuss their project in small groups.
○ Call on students to share their observations and ideas with the class.

ANSWER KEY
Answers will vary.

EXPANSION ACTIVITY: A Silent Drama
○ Put students in pairs to write a dialogue of about 10 sentences. Instruct them to include a hand gesture or some body language with every sentence.
○ Students may write the dialogue on any subject or use one of the following topics: a scary story, a disagreement about housework, the best route to school, or something one person loves, but the other hates.
○ Call on pairs of students to perform their dialogue for the class—but without talking. They will only use nonverbal communication.
○ Call on other students for guesses about what the dialogue was about. Encourage students to make their guesses as detailed as possible.
○ Next, have the pair read their dialogue aloud, this time using both words and nonverbal communication.

○ Repeat for each pair of students.
○ As a class, discuss which details were easy to guess, and which were difficult.

EXPANSION ACTIVITY: Koko and Michael

○ Photocopy and distribute the worksheet *Koko and Michael* on page BLM 6.
○ Have students read the information and answer the questions.
○ Go over the answers with the class.

ANSWER KEY

1. True; 2. False; 3. False; 4. True; 5. False; 6. False; 7. True; 8. False

CHAPTER 4 NUTRITION

In Part 1, students will read an article about nutrition myths. In Part 2, students will listen to three people talking about food and nutrition. In Part 4, students will listen to a radio program about the diet in the Mediterranean region. In Part 5, students will listen to an academic lecture on nutrition. Finally, students will work in small groups to plan a nutritious meal.

VOCABULARY

after all	cuisine	kimchi	safeguard
alter	decrease	life expectancy	sedentary
anecdote	diet	linked	simple carbohydrates
antioxidant	endorsed	maintain	sound
be associated with	energy	milligram	statistics
burns	essential	mineral	store
chronic illness	ethnic food	moderation	such as
collaborate	gingko	myth	supplements
complex carbohydrates	gram	nutrients	theory
concentrated	herbs	nutrition	to tell you the truth
consume	in abundance	phytochemicals	vitamin
cover	incidence	profound	well-balanced
critical	intrigue	promote	

LISTENING STRATEGIES

Listening for Numerical Information
Guessing the Meaning from Context: *Such As*
Previewing: Asking Questions Before You Listen
Getting the Main Ideas from the Introduction
Listening for Categories and Definitions

CRITICAL THINKING STRATEGIES

Separating Facts from Opinions (Part 2)
Comparing Sources of Information (Part 5)
Note: Strategy in bold is highlighted in the Student Book.

MECHANICS OF LISTENING AND SPEAKING

Language Functions: Asking for More Information: Reasons
Asking for More Information: Examples
Giving More Information: Reasons or Examples
Pronunciation: Reduced Forms of Words: Questions with *Do* and *Did*
Words In Phrases: Noun Phrases for Types of Food

SPEAKING STRATEGY

Taking Turns

TEST-TAKING STRATEGY

Listening for Reasons

CHAPTER 4 Nutrition

Chapter 4 Opener, page 111
○ Direct students' attention to the photo and chapter title. Go over the directions and questions.
○ Put students in pairs to share their ideas.
○ Call on students to share their ideas with the class.

PART ① INTRODUCTION NUTRITION FACTS AND FICTION, PAGES 112–115

A. Thinking Ahead
○ Direct students' attention to the photos. Ask: *What foods do you see?*
○ Go over the directions and the questions.
○ Have students fill in the bubble for *True* or *False*.

ANSWER KEY
Answers will vary. Students will review their answers in Activity E on page 114.

B. Discussion
○ Go over the directions and the questions.
○ Have students discuss the questions with a partner.
○ Call on students to share their ideas with the class.

ANSWER KEY
Answers will vary.

EXPANSION ACTIVITY: Vote with Your Feet
○ Write *Agree* on one side of the board and *Disagree* on the other.
○ Explain the activity. You will say a sentence and students should stand near the word that expresses their opinion.
○ Call a group of students to the board. Say *The American diet is not healthy.* Remind students to stand near *Agree* or *Disagree*.

○ Ask students to explain their position.
○ Say other sentences. Use your own or the ones below. You may want to have different groups of students come to the board.
  You should eat more protein than carbohydrates.
  It doesn't matter what you eat; it's more important how much you eat.
  You should stop eating when you are really full.
  All fats are bad for you.

C. Reading
○ Direct students' attention to the article on page 113.
○ Go over the directions and the question.
○ Have students read the article and think about the question.
○ Ask: *What are some myths about nutrition?*

Academic Note
○ Remind students of the importance of previewing an article. Elicit ideas for what students can preview in this article (e.g., *title, bold-faced material, vocabulary words, source information*).

D. Vocabulary Check
○ Go over the directions.
○ Have students write the words or phrases on the lines and then compare answers with a partner.
○ Go over the answers with the class.

TOEFL® iBT Tip

TOEFL iBT Tip 1: The TOEFL iBT tests the ability to determine the meaning of words in context and comprehend the overall gist of a lecture or conversation.

○ Point out that the activity *Vocabulary Check* will help students improve their vocabulary by interpreting a word based on context and using the logic of grammar.

○ By reading vocabulary in a text, students can reinforce what they will hear and use in speaking tasks. This will also help students prepare for the integrated reading/listening/speaking task.

ANSWER KEY

1. critical; 2. well-balanced diet; 3. simple carbohydrate; 4. nutrients; 5. stores; 6. sedentary; 7. gram

E. Discussion
○ Go over the directions.
○ Have students discuss the questions in small groups.
○ Call on students to share their ideas with the class.

ANSWER KEY

1. Answers will vary. 2–6. In Activity A, all of the sentences were false.

F. Journal Writing
○ Go over the directions.
○ Explain that this is a quick-writing activity and does not have to be perfect. Point out that journal writing can be a warm-up to a more structured writing assignment, helping to generate ideas.
○ Set a time limit of five minutes.
○ Put students in pairs to read or talk about their writing.

PART ② SOCIAL LANGUAGE
RACHEL'S HEALTH PLAN, PAGES 115–118

Before Listening
A. Thinking Ahead
○ Go over the directions and the questions.
○ Have students complete the chart and then compare ideas with a partner.
○ Call on students to share their ideas with the class.

ANSWER KEY
Answers will vary.

B. Vocabulary Preparation
○ Go over the directions.
○ Have students match the definitions with the words in red.
○ Go over the answers with the class.

ANSWER KEY
1. c; 2. f; 3. d; 4. a; 5. b; 6. e

EXPANSION ACTIVITY: Flash Cards
○ Bring index cards to class, or assign students to bring some in.
○ Explain that flash cards are a good way to review vocabulary. Tell students to write new vocabulary words on one side and definitions or pictures on the other.
○ Have students use the index cards to create flashcards for any words they want to remember in the chapter.

Listening

🔊🎧 A. Listening for the Main Idea

❍ Go over the directions and the questions.
❍ Play the video or audio program.
❍ Ask students: *Does Rachel worry about eating healthy food? Why or why not?*

Audio Script

Rachel: Hey, hi, what's up?
Ashley and Mike: Good, just hanging out.
Rachel: Hey, Ashley, that looks good. What is it?
Ashley: Uh . . . chili soup.
Rachel: That looks so good. What's the problem?
Ashley: Oh, these things are never spicy enough . . . And there's no hot sauce . . .
Mike: Hey, man, I told you—you should carry your own bottle of hot sauce 'cause you love it so much!
Ashley: Yeah. Man, do I miss my mom's kimchi! You ever had that?
Mike: Nope.
Rachel: No way! I don't like spicy food. You know that!
Ashley: Well, hot stuff's good for you—a lot better than some of the stuff people usually eat, like fast food.
Mike: Hey, that's right. Remember, we heard about this, in our nutrition class. Uh, a study that said Mexican food was bad for you, but they were studying, you know, the stuff that, you know, you get in a fast food restaurant, not the real thing.
Rachel: Actually, I *do* like those fast food *tacos* . . . they're not too spicy . . .
Mike: Anyway, *real* Mexican cuisine is supposed to be very healthy.
Rachel: How come?
Mike: Well, you, you get a lot of rice, and beans, and corn, and, ah, lotsa complex carbohydrates . . . not too much meat or fat . . . and, uh, the uh, chili pepper is supposed to have a lotta vitamin C.
Rachel: Well, I don't worry too much about eating healthy food anyway 'cause I take vitamins.
Ashley: Like what?
Rachel: Well . . . Uh, every day I take 1000 milligrams of vitamin C, and, uh . . . 1000 milligrams of E, B complex—
Mike: That sounds like a lot!
Rachel: I take herbs, too.
Ashley: Such as?
Rachel: Ginkgo, ginseng—
Mike: What are those for?

Rachel: They give you energy and help your brain, I think.
Mike: You don't sound too sure.
Ashley: Are there studies that prove this?
Rachel: To tell you the truth, I don't really know, but I *did* get an "A" on that nutrition exam we had last week!
Ashley: Ah! So, maybe they do some good after all!

ANSWER KEY

Rachel doesn't worry about eating healthy food because she takes vitamins and herbs.

🔊🎧 B. Listening for Opinions

❍ Go over the directions.
❍ Have students match the topic with comments or opinions as you play the video or audio program a second time.
❍ Put students in pairs to compare answers.
❍ Go over the answers with the class.

Audio Script

❍ Use the script for Activity A above.

ANSWER KEY

1. e; 2. c; 3. a; 4. b; 5. d

CRITICAL THINKING STRATEGY: Separating Facts from Opinions

❍ When listening, it's very important to separate facts from opinions. Speakers often try to make their opinions sound like facts or make facts sound like opinions.
❍ *Facts* are statements about the world. They are either true or false. *Opinions* are a person's feelings or thoughts about the world. They are neither true nor false.
❍ Facts can be proved or disproved with evidence, and they do not make judgments of value.

TOEFL® iBT Tip

TOEFL iBT Tip 2: To answer the pragmatic understanding questions on the TOEFL iBT, students need to recognize a speaker's attitude, degree of certainty, motivation, or purpose.

○ Point out that the activity *Listening for Opinions* will help students to distinguish between facts and opinions, providing clues to purpose and motivation.

○ Students will also be able to apply this skill to the independent speaking task, on which they must state and defend an opinion.

C. Listening for Details

○ Go over the directions.
○ Have students fill in the blanks as you play the video or audio program.
○ Go over the answers with the class.

Audio Script

Rachel: Well, I don't worry too much about eating healthy food anyway 'cause I take vitamins.
Ashley: Like what?
Rachel: Well . . . Uh, every day I take 1000 milligrams of vitamin C, and, uh, 1000 milligrams of E, B complex—
Mike: That sounds like a lot!
Rachel: I take herbs, too.
Ashley: Such as?
Rachel: Ginkgo, ginseng—
Mike: What are those for?
Rachel: They give you energy and help your brain, I think.

ANSWER KEY

1. vitamins; 2. 1,000; 3. C; 4. milligrams; 5. B; 6. herbs; 7. gingko; 8. energy

EXPANSION ACTIVITY: Asking about Details

○ Play the audio program for Activity C again. Have students listen and take notes on other details.
○ Have students write two questions about details (e.g., *What does Ashley miss?*).
○ Divide the class into an even number of teams.
○ Put two teams together to challenge each other by asking questions. For each question asked that isn't answered, the team that is asking scores a point.

After Listening
A. Information Gap

○ Go over the directions and the questions.
○ Put students in pairs. Have Student A in each pair turn to page 203 and Student B turn to page 207.
○ Have students take turns asking and answering questions about the labels.
○ If necessary, go over the answers with the class.

ANSWER KEY

Student A's questions:
IU; 100 IU; pyridoxine; calcium; 10 mg
Student B's questions:
thiamin; Vitamin B-2; 7.2 mg; zinc; 20 mg

B. Discussion

○ Go over the directions.
○ Have students discuss the questions in small groups.
○ Call on students to share their ideas with the class.

ANSWER KEY

Answers will vary.

PART ③ THE MECHANICS OF LISTENING AND SPEAKING, PAGES 118–123

LANGUAGE FUNCTIONS: Asking for More Information: Reasons

○ Go over the information in the box.
○ Ask comprehension questions: *What is one way to get more information when you don't understand something? What are two ways to ask for reasons?*
○ Ask students to identify the expressions that are more formal and those that are more informal. (The phrases at the top of the list are more informal, and the ones at the bottom are more formal.)

A. Asking for More Information: Reasons

○ Go over the directions and the example.
○ Have students write the words and expressions on the lines as you play the audio program.
○ Go over the answers with the class.

Audio Script

1. **A:** Chili pepper is supposed to be good for you.
   B: Why?
   A: It has a lot of vitamin C.
2. **A:** Eating too much sugar is supposed to be bad for you.
   B: Why do you say that?
   A: It can cause tooth decay.
3. **A:** Weight training is more important than eating a lot of protein.
   B: How come?
   A: It can help you build muscles.
4. **A:** I think gingko is good for you.
   B: What do you mean?
   A: It can give you energy.
5. **A:** Eating fat can make you fat.
   B: Excuse me, but what do you mean by that?
   A: Fat has a lot of calories.

B. Asking for More Information

○ Go over the directions.
○ Have students fill in the correct bubbles as you play the audio program. Repeat the audio program if necessary.
○ Go over the answers with the class.

Audio Script

1. **A:** Everybody needs carbohydrates.
   B: How come?
   A: They give you energy
2. **A:** I think it's important to take supplements.
   B: Excuse me, but why do you say that?
   A: Because most people don't eat a well-balanced diet.
3. **A:** Mexican food is very healthy.
   B: Whaddya mean?
   A: Well, you get a lot of complex carbohydrates.
4. **A:** Eating fat can make you fat.
   B: Excuse me, but what do you mean by that?
   A: Fat has a lot of calories.
5. **A:** Broccoli is better for you than iceberg lettuce.
   B: Whaddya mean?
   A: Broccoli has more vitamins and minerals.

Asking for More Information: Examples

○ Go over the information in the box.
○ Ask questions: *What is another way to get more information on a topic? What are some informal ways to ask for examples? What are some more formal ways?* (Expressions at the top of the list are more informal.)

C. Asking for More Information: Examples

○ Go over the directions and the examples.
○ Have students work in pairs, taking turns talking about something they like or liked or something they do or did, and asking for an example.
○ Walk around to monitor the activity and provide help as needed.

Giving More Information: Reasons or Examples

○ Go over the information in the box.
○ Ask comprehension questions: *How can you introduce a reason? How can you introduce an example?*
○ Point out that the phrase *That's why* is used in a new sentence after a reason, while the other expressions for giving reasons are used before the reason.

TOEFL® iBT Tip

TOEFL iBT Tip 3: The TOEFL iBT independent speaking tasks require examinees to express and justify likes and dislikes, state opinions and support them, make recommendations and justify them, and so on.

○ Point out that the activity *Giving More Information: Reasons or Examples* will help students to isolate important vocabulary that they hear and use it in response to a speaking prompt.

○ The phrases *such as, like,* and *for example* will help students to support their statements by giving examples and reasons.

D. Giving More Information: Reasons or Examples

○ Go over the directions, examples, and topics.
○ Have students work in pairs, taking turns making statements and asking for more information.
○ Walk around to monitor the activity and provide help as needed.

🎧 PRONUNCIATION: Reduced Forms of Words: Questions with *Do* and *Did*

○ Go over the information in the box and play the audio program.
○ Ask comprehension questions: *What is the reduced form of* What do you mean? *What is the long form of* Howja get here?

🎧 E. Reduced Forms of Words: Questions with *Do* and *Did*

○ Go over the directions.
○ Have students complete the conversation with the long forms as you play the audio program.
○ Put students in pairs to compare conversations.
○ Go over the answers with the class.

Audio Script

A: Whereja say you were going?
B: I said I was going to get some lunch at the Student Union.
A: Whydya want to eat at the Student Union? The food is terrible.
B: I like the chili soup there.
A: Whaja say?
B: I like the chili.
A: Whaja mean? That stuff's terrible!
B: That's *your* opinion. I happen to like it.

ANSWER KEY

1. Where did you; 2. Why do you; 3. What did you;
4. What do you

EXPANSION ACTIVITY: Dictation

❍ Tell students you are going to dictate five sentences. Have students write the sentences you dictate. Say each sentence three times. Create your own or use these examples:

What do you eat to help you with weight training?

Can you give an example of one kind of fat that isn't harmful?

Why do you say that organic food is better for the environment?

What cuisine do you think is the most balanced?

Can you tell me what you mean by "empty calories"?

❍ Have students compare sentences with a partner.

❍ Ask volunteers to write the sentences on the board.

WORDS IN PHRASES: Noun Phrases for Types of Food

❍ Go over the information in the box.

❍ Ask comprehension questions: *What is a noun phrase? What is an example of an adjective + noun combination? What about a noun + noun combination?*

EXPANSION ACTIVITY: Using Noun Phrases

❍ Have students choose four noun phrases from the box and write sentences using each one.

❍ Have students read their sentences in pairs.

❍ Call on students to read their sentences to the class.

Put It Together
Asking For and Giving More Information

❍ Go over the directions and the examples.

❍ Direct students' attention to the topics.

❍ Model the activity. Call on two students to demonstrate. Introduce a topic by expressing an opinion (*My favorite junk food is French fries*). Prompt students to ask for more information and express their own ideas.

❍ Put students in groups of three or four to talk about the topics. Remind students to ask for and give reasons and examples, and to use noun phrases if possible.

❍ Walk around to monitor the activity and provide help as needed.

EXPANSION ACTIVITY: Guessing the Category

❍ Model the activity. Tell the class, *I'm thinking of a category of things or people.* Write the phrase *movie stars* on a piece of paper.

❍ Have students take turns asking you for examples of the category. Remind them to use expressions from the Language Functions box on page 120.

❍ Give well-known examples of movie stars such as *Tom Cruise, Zhang Ziyi,* etc.

❍ After you give each example, let the person who asked for the example try to guess the category. When someone guesses correctly, show the piece of paper.

❍ Divide the class into small groups and have them take turns guessing each other's categories. Suggest possible categories like *old-fashioned clothing, sad movies, romantic places,* or have students make up their own.

PART ④ BROADCAST ENGLISH
THE MEDITERRANEAN DIET, PAGES 124–129

Before Listening
A. Brainstorming

❍ Go over the directions.

❍ Have students write the names of the countries they know on the chart.

❍ Put students in pairs to compare maps.

❍ Direct students' attention to the photos on page 125. Have students write the names of other Mediterranean foods on the chart.

❍ Call on students to share their ideas with the class.

ANSWER KEY

Answers may vary.

Albania
Algeria
Bosnia and Herzegovina
Croatia
Cyprus
Egypt
France
Greece
Israel
Italy
Lebanon
Libya
Monaco
Morocco
Slovenia
Spain
Syria
Tunisia
Turkey
Yugoslavia
eggplant
olive oil
lemon
olives
pasta
tomatoes
mint
artichokes
garlic
bulgur/cracked wheat
grapes

B. Thinking Ahead
○ Go over the directions.
○ Have students discuss the question in pairs.
○ Have students fill in the bubbles for *True* or *False* and compare answers with their partners.
○ Call on students to share their ideas with the class.

ANSWER KEY

Answers may vary. Students will learn more about the diet as they listen. Correct answers follow.
The Mediterranean diet is healthy because it has a lot of fruits and vegetables and healthy fats.
1. T; 2. T; 3. F; 4. F; 5. T

C. Vocabulary Preparation
○ Go over the directions.
○ Have students write the correct words or phrases on the lines.
○ Go over the answers with the class.

ANSWER KEY

1. intrigues; 2. life expectancy; 3. consume; 4. in abundance; 5. altered; 6. endorsed; 7. incidence; 8. safeguarding; 9. sound; 10. linked

---

EXPANSION ACTIVITY: Beanbag Toss
○ Tell students they have one minute to review the vocabulary.
○ After one minute, ask students to close their books.
○ Explain that you will call on a student and toss a beanbag or ball. You will say one of the definitions, and the students should respond with the vocabulary word or phrase and throw the beanbag back.
○ Call on a student and toss the beanbag, saying *changed.* Elicit an answer from the student (*altered*) and have them toss the beanbag or ball back to you.
○ Repeat with other students until all have had a chance to participate. This is a fast-paced activity.

Listening
🎧 A. Listening for the Main Idea: Section 1
○ Go over the directions.
○ Have students write the answer to the question as you play the audio program.
○ Have students compare answers with a partner.
○ Go over the answer with the students.

Audio Script

Host: Take a trip to the Mediterranean, and you'll probably notice something more than the flavorful food. For decades, researchers have linked this region with good health. One nation that stood out is Greece, where scientists in the 1960s found one of the highest rates of adult life expectancy on earth.

Studies of the whole Mediterranean basin showed a lower incidence there of chronic illness, such as cancer and heart disease, than in northern Europe, Japan, and the United States. Less stress, fewer cars, and more walking, as well as a cleaner environment contributed to the atmosphere of well-being. But it was the Mediterranean *diet* that intrigued researchers most. People there consume on average lower amounts of harmful fats, and plentiful portions of grains and tender, fresh vegetables, and fruits.

You'll find wooden carts overflowing with them in most any neighborhood marketplace, this one in the heart of Naples in southern Italy. There are deep purple eggplants ready for the roasting, plump, fruity tomatoes ready for anything, and pungent cloves of garlic, nature's way of drawing us to the dinner table— and just possibly, safeguarding us from disease. Tucked away in these vegetables and fruits at the microscopic level, scientists have identified a swirl of natural protective ingredients, such as antioxidants, that can help prevent illness. It's a whole secret pharmacy in your food. And worldwide, hundreds of studies show populations that consume fruits and vegetables in abundance have a much lower rate of cancer and other serious diseases.

ANSWER KEY

Their diet is healthier, with lower amounts of harmful fats and lots of grains, vegetables, and fruits.

EXPANSION ACTIVITY: The Okinawan Diet

❍ Photocopy and distribute the worksheet *The Okinawan Diet* on page BLM 7.
❍ Have students read the information and answer the questions.
❍ Go over the answers with the class.

ANSWER KEY

1. F; 2. F; 3. T; 4. F; 5. T; 6. T; 7. F; 8. F; 9. F; 10. F

🎧 B. Listening for Details: Section 1

❍ Go over the directions.
❍ Have students check the appropriate column as you play the audio program.
❍ Go over the answers with the class.

Audio Script

Use the script for Activity A above.

ANSWER KEY

	Mediterranean People	Non-Mediterranean People
have less stress	✔	
walk less		✔
drive more		✔
eat a lot of fat		✔
eat a lot of vegetables	✔	
live in a clean environment	✔	

TEST-TAKING STRATEGY: Listening for Reasons

❍ Go over the information in the box.
❍ Ask comprehension questions: *What is an anecdote? What are statistics? Why do people sometimes include this information?*

TOEFL® iBT Tip

TOEFL iBT Tip 4: It will be important for examinees to determine a speaker's attitude or purpose, as well as reasons that are presented in a conversation or lecture.

○ Remind students that the listening strategy *Listening for Reasons* will be helpful for finding important details and for identifying a speaker's purpose or opinion.

○ On the TOEFL iBT, a content question may appear in the following formats:
   Why does the speaker mention _____?
   Why is _____ *important?*

🎧 C. Listening for Reasons: Section 1
○ Go over the directions.
○ Have students write at least two reasons why the Mediterranean diet is healthy as you play the audio program.
○ Go over the answers with the class.

Audio Script
○ Use the script for Activity A on page 74 of the Teacher's Edition.

ANSWER KEY
It's low in harmful kinds of fat.
It has a lot of grains, fruits, and vegetables.
It has a lot of antioxidants.

🎧 D. Listening for Details: Section 1
○ Go over the directions.
○ Have students write the names of fruits and vegetables as you play the audio program.
○ Go over the answers with the class.

Audio Script
Host: You'll find wooden carts overflowing with them in most any neighborhood marketplace, such as this one in the heart of Naples in southern Italy. There are deep purple eggplants ready for the roasting, plump, fruity tomatoes ready for anything, and pungent cloves of garlic, nature's way of drawing us to the dinner table—and just possibly, safeguarding us from disease. Tucked away in these vegetables and fruits at the microscopic level, scientists have identified a swirl of natural protective ingredients, such as antioxidants, that can help prevent illness. It's a whole secret pharmacy in your food. And worldwide, hundreds of studies show populations that consume fruits and vegetables in abundance have a much lower rate of cancer and other serious diseases.

ANSWER KEY
eggplant, tomatoes, garlic

🎧 E. Listening for the Main Idea: Section 2
○ Go over the directions.
○ Have students write the answer to the question as you play the audio program.
○ Go over the answer with the class.

Audio Script
Byars: All the way from the mouth on down through the stomach, in the colorectum, and also lung cancer and many other internal organ cancers, uh, risk is reduced by 50 percent or so, for people who eat five or more servings a day of fruits and vegetables, compared to many people who are out there who eat two or less a day. And I think that's a very important difference.
Host: With cancer now responsible for a fifth of all deaths in America, the fight against it is shifting to prevention. Scientists estimate that what we eat accounts for at least a third of all cancers. So a sound diet is now cited as powerful protection, and Americans are becoming more conscious about the benefits of healthy eating.

The National Cancer Institute, the surgeon general, and all major health authorities have endorsed the five-a-day recommendation: consume at least five daily servings of fruits and vegetables. A serving is about a half a cup of vegetables, or a whole piece of fruit. Americans typically eat only about two to three servings per day. Compare that to the Mediterranean, where, in southern Italy, for example, the average person eats a many as *11* servings per day.

Dr. Anna Ferraluzzi, of the National Institute of Nutrition, in Rome:

Ferraluzzi: Another aspect is that if you eat fruits and vegetables, you eat less of something else. Uh, if you go back to our Mediterranean diet, we start our meals . . . we have several-course meals—it's a classical one—and the first, uh, dish is a pasta dish or a soup dish, so this will occupy part of your appetite and your stomach space so that you probably will have a smaller helping of the second, uh, plate. And the second plate will be meat or another animal-based, uh, product. So the whole thing is linked together. Um, you definitely need also to have a d-di-uh-diet which is varied, and uh, the, the basic composition of even of your fruits and vegetables still be such that it arrives on your dish without having been altered too much.

ANSWER KEY

to prevent cancer deaths

LISTENING STRATEGY: Listening for Numerical Information

○ Go over the information in the box.
○ Ask: *What are some words you should listen for?*

TOEFL® iBT Tip

TOEFL iBT Tip 5: The TOEFL iBT measures the ability to understand the main idea or important details of a conversation or a lecture.

○ Point out that numbers, percentages, or other statistics that are presented in a lecture or conversation are important details that students will need to note.

○ The listening strategy *Listening for Numerical Information* will help students improve their overall basic comprehension skills.

F. Listening for Numerical Information: Section 2

○ Go over the directions.
○ Have students write the numerical words and expressions as you play the audio program.
○ Have students compare ideas with a partner.
○ Go over the answers with the class.

Audio Script

Byars: All the way from the mouth on down through the stomach, the colorectum, and also lung cancer and many other internal organ cancers, uh, risk is reduced by 50 percent or so, for people who eat five or more servings a day of fruits and vegetables, compared to many people who are out there who eat two or less a day. And I think that's a very important difference.
Host: With cancer now responsible for a fifth of all deaths in America, the fight against it is shifting to prevention. Scientists estimate that what we eat accounts for at least a third of all cancers.

ANSWER KEY

1. fifty percent; 2. five or more; 3. two or less; 4. fifth; 5. third

LISTENING STRATEGY: Guessing the Meaning from Context: *Such As*
○ Go over the information in the box.
○ Ask questions: *What is one way to guess the meaning of a new word? What expression often introduces an example?*

🎧 G. Guessing the Meaning from Context: *Such As*
○ Go over the directions.
○ Have students write the meanings of the words as you play the audio program.
○ Go over the answers with the class.

Audio Script
1. Studies of the whole Mediterranean basin showed a lower incidence there of chronic illness, such as cancer and heart disease, than in northern Europe, Japan, and the United States.
2. Tucked away in these vegetables and fruits at the microscopic level, scientists have identified a swirl of natural protective ingredients, such as antioxidants, that can help prevent illness.

ANSWER KEY
1. diseases such as cancer and heart disease; 2. natural protective ingredients

After Listening
A. Discussion
○ Go over the directions and the questions.
○ Put students in small groups to discuss the questions.
○ Call on students to share their ideas with the class.

ANSWER KEY
Answers will vary.

B. Discussing Your Predictions
○ Go over the directions.
○ Have students work with their partners from Activity B on page 125 to look at their previous answers and change them if necessary.
○ Call on students to tell the class which predictions were right and wrong.

PART ⑤ ACADEMIC ENGLISH
BASIC PRINCIPLES OF NUTRITION, PAGES 130–140

Before Listening
A. Thinking Ahead
○ Go over the directions.
○ Have students discuss the questions in small groups.
○ Call on students to share their ideas with the class.

ANSWER KEY
Answers will vary.

LISTENING STRATEGY: Previewing: Asking Questions Before You Listen
○ Go over the information in the box.
○ Ask: *Why should you ask questions before you listen?*

B. Previewing: Asking Questions Before You Listen
○ Go over the directions.
○ Direct students' attention to the outline on page 132. Have students write three questions about nutrition.
○ Have students compare their questions with a partner.
○ Call on students to tell the class one of their questions.

C. Vocabulary Preparation
○ Go over the directions.
○ Have students complete the sentences with words or phrases from the box and then compare answers with a partner.
○ Go over the answers with the class.

Listening

LISTENING STRATEGY: Getting the Main Ideas from the Introduction

○ Go over the information in the box.
○ Ask: *Where in the lecture do speakers often tell the main idea?*

TOEFL® iBT Tip

TOEFL iBT Tip 6: The basic understanding questions on the TOEFL iBT will require students to listen for the main idea, details, organization, and content of a lecture.

○ Point out that the listening strategy *Getting the Main Ideas from the Introduction* will help students to identify the main idea or topic of a lecture.

○ Mention that students can use the main idea to anticipate vocabulary and details that may appear later in the lecture.

A. Getting the Main Ideas from the Introduction

○ Go over the directions and the questions.
○ Have students answer the questions as you play the audio program.
○ Put students in pairs to compare answers.
○ Go over the answers with the class.

Audio Script

Lecturer: Hello. Did everyone have a nice weekend? Good. Today I'm going to discuss some basic principles of nutrition. I'm going to cover the nutrients in food, the connection between nutrition and health, and how to plan a healthy diet. I'm also going to give you an overview of the nutritional aspects of two ethnic cuisines.

B. Taking Notes: Using an Outline

○ Go over the directions.
○ Have students fill in the outline as you play the audio program. Play each section twice.
○ Have students compare notes with a partner.

Audio Script

Section 1

Lecturer: Hello. Did everyone have a nice weekend? Good. Today I'm going to discuss some basic principles of nutrition. I'm going to cover the nutrients in food, the connection between nutrition and health, and how to plan a healthy diet. I'm also going to give you an overview of the nutritional aspects of two ethnic cuisines.

Let's start with the principles of good nutrition. The food we eat, our diet, has a profound effect on our health. Good nutrition is essential for good health, but what is nutrition? Nutrition involves the nutrients in food and the body's handling of those nutrients. Nutrients are substances that are obtained from foods and used in the body to provide energy and to promote growth, maintenance, and repair of the body's tissues.

There are six classes of nutrients. They include carbohydrates, fats, protein, vitamins, minerals, and water. The carbohydrates include sugars, starches, and most types of dietary fiber. They are found in foods like breads, cereals, grains, and fruit. The fats include lard, oils, and cholesterol. Carbohydrates and fats provide the body with energy. Proteins are used to build and repair body tissues and are found in meat, milk, eggs, and beans. Vitamins and minerals are needed for proper body functioning.

Section 2

Lecturer: Many studies have shown the connections between nutrition and disease. In fact, nutrition plays a role in four of the ten leading causes of illness and death in the United States. Diseases associated with poor nutrition include heart disease, high blood pressure, diabetes, and obesity. Government and other agencies have developed diet recommendations to prevent disease, such as the Dietary Guidelines for Americans.

These guidelines are:
1. Eat a variety of foods.
2. Maintain a healthy weight.
3. Choose a diet low in fat, especially saturated fat and cholesterol.
4. Choose a diet with plenty of vegetable, fruits, and grain products.
5. Use sugars only in moderation.
6. Use salt and sodium in moderation.
7. If you drink alcoholic beverages, do so in moderation.

Section 3

Lecturer: Now, let's move on to the second main point of today's lecture: planning a healthy diet. To plan a healthy diet, people first need to understand the five food groups. Foods can be divided into groups, each group containing foods that are similar in nutrient content. The five food groups are: Grain products like breads and cereals; vegetables; fruits; dairy products like milk and cheese; and meats, including fish, poultry, and protein substitutes like beans.

The second part of planning a healthy diet is understanding diet planning principles. It is not difficult to eat a healthy diet if you take the time to learn about nutrition and use the principles of balance, variety, and moderation. Balance means that you eat the right amount of foods from each of the food groups. For example, eating a diet that contained only milk and bread wouldn't be healthy. Variety is a similar concept. For good health it is best to select foods from each of the groups each day. Moderation means that we should eat only as much food as we need and not overeat.

The third part of planning a healthy diet is smart shopping. Read food labels when shopping to help you make healthy food choices. Choose whole grain and enriched breads and cereals. Fresh green and yellow-orange vegetables are important, as well as yellow-orange and citrus fruits. Legumes (beans and peas) are nutritious and inexpensive. Select lean meats, fish and poultry with visible fat removed. Low fat milk and milk products are recommended over full fat versions.

Section 4

Lecturer: In the last part of today's lecture, we're going to take a look at the nutritional aspects of certain ethnic diets. Food has many meanings for people—it is not only a means of providing nutrients for the body. People eat for pleasure, and as part of family and social situations. One of the greatest influences on eating habits is culture. People often experience feelings of pleasure and comfort when eating their traditional cultural foods. Ethnic diets are characteristic of particular racial, ethnic, and cultural groups.

The term foodways can be used when discussing ethnic diets. Foodways describe the food habits, as well as the customs and beliefs about food in a particular culture.

There are positive and negative aspects to all types of diets, and any type of diet can be healthy as long as proper food choices are made.

Here are some examples of two ethnic diets: Mediterranean and Chinese.

People from countries that border the Mediterranean Sea, such as Greece and Italy, consume a diet which has been called the Mediterranean diet. This diet includes seafood, meats—especially lamb, chicken, and beef—cheese, fruits, and vegetables. This diet is quite high in fat; however, most of the fat comes from olive oil. Consuming a diet rich in olive oil has been associated with a lower risk of heart disease and the Mediterranean diet is considered to be a heart-healthy diet.

Chinese meals are built around rice, contain small amounts of meat, seafood, poultry, and eggs mixed with vegetables, and usually include soups and tea. The Chinese diet is low in fat and high in fiber. Chinese foods tend to be high in salt, which is not recommended. When the salt is reduced, Chinese food is a healthy diet choice.

So, in conclusion, good nutrition is essential to good health. Knowing what's in food and following a few basic guidelines can lead to better health not only today, but in the future.

ANSWER KEY

Section 1

I. Introduction to Nutrients
- A. Definition: <u>substances from food, provide body with energy and help growth, maintenance, and repair of body tissues</u>
- B. Classes of nutrients
  1. <u>Carbohydrates Examples: sugars, starches, Most types of dietary fiber, breads, cereals, grains, fruits</u> (Purpose: give energy)
  2. Fats Examples: oil, <u>lard, cholesterol</u> (Purpose: <u>Give energy</u>)
  3. Proteins—build <u>and repair body tissue</u>
  4. Vitamins <u>needed for proper body functioning</u>
  5. Minerals <u>needed for proper body functioning</u>
  6. Water

Section 2

II. The Connection Between Nutrition and Disease
- A. Nutrition plays a role in four out of ten causes of <u>illness and death in the United States</u>
- B. Diseases include heart disease, high blood pressure, diabetes, and <u>obesity</u>
- C. The government has developed <u>diet recommendations</u> in order to <u>prevent disease</u>

III. Dietary Guidelines for Americans
- A. Eat <u>a variety of foods</u>
- B. Maintain <u>a healthy weight</u>
- C. Choose <u>a diet low in fat, saturated fat, and cholesterol</u>
- D. Choose <u>a diet with plenty of vegetables, fruits, and grain products</u>
- E. Use <u>sugars only in moderation</u>
- F. Use salt and sodium only in <u>moderation</u>
- G. If you drink <u>alcoholic beverages, do so in moderation</u>

Section 3

IV. Planning a Healthy Diet
- A. Five food groups
  1. <u>breads, cereals and other grain products</u>
  2. <u>vegetables</u>
  3. Fruits
  4. dairy products like <u>milk and cheese</u>
  5. <u>meat, poultry, fish and beans</u>
- B. Diet planning principles
  1. Balance: eat right amount of foods from each group
  2. Variety: <u>select foods from each group each day</u>

  3. Moderation: <u>eat only as much as you need, don't overeat</u>
- C. Smart food shopping
  1. Read <u>food labels—look for healthy food choices</u>
  2. Choose <u>whole grain and enriched breads and cereals</u>
  3. Important fruits and vegetables are <u>fresh green and yellow-orange vegetables, yellow-orange and citrus fruits</u>
  4. Legumes are <u>nutritious and inexpensive (beans and peas)</u>
  5. Select lean meats, fish, and poultry, and low-fat milk products

Section 4

V. Nutritional Aspects of Ethnic Diets
- A. The meaning of food
  1. people eat for pleasure; to be part of family and social situations
  2. culture influences eating habits
     a. eating traditional cultural foods makes people feel <u>pleasure and comfort</u>
     b. ethnic diets are characteristic of <u>particular racial, ethnic and cultural groups</u>
     c. the term "foodways" means <u>food habits, customs, and beliefs in a particular culture</u>
- B. Mediterranean
  1. the diet includes <u>seafood, meat, cheese, fruits, and vegetables</u>
  2. most of the fat comes from <u>olive oil</u>
  3. people consider the diet to be <u>a heart-healthy diet</u>
- C. Chinese
  1. the diet includes <u>rice, small amounts of meat, seafood, poultry and eggs mixed with vegetables, soups and tea</u>
  2. it's low in <u>fat</u> and high in <u>fiber</u>
  3. it's a good diet when <u>salt is reduced</u>

LISTENING STRATEGY: Listening for Categories and Definitions

○ Go over the information in the box.
○ Ask questions: *What are some expressions that introduce categories? What are some expressions that introduce definitions or explanations?*

C. Listening for Categories and Definitions

○ Go over the directions.
○ Have students write the answers as you play the audio program again.
○ Have students compare answers with a partner.
○ Go over the answers with the class.

Audio Script

Use the script for Activity B on page 78 of the Teacher's Edition.

ANSWER KEY

1. six; 2. they are similar in nutrient content (have the same nutrients); 3. eat the right amount of food from each of the food groups

D. Checking Your Notes

○ Go over the directions.
○ Have students check their notes as you play the audio program again.
○ Have students compare outlines with a partner.
○ Go over the answers with the class.

Audio Script

Use the script for Activity B on page 78 of the Teacher's Edition.

ANSWER KEY

Use the outline for Activity B on page 80 of the Teacher's Edition.

After Listening

A. Using Your Notes

○ Go over the directions and the questions.
○ Have students discuss the questions in small groups.
○ Call on students to share their answers with the class.

ANSWER KEY

Answers may vary.

1. Nutrients are substances from food that provide body with energy, help growth, maintenance, and repair of body tissues, and include carbohydrates (e.g., grains, fruits), fats (e.g., oil), protein (e.g., meat), vitamins (e.g., vitamin C), minerals (e.g., calcium), and water.
2. Good nutrition can help prevent disease.
3. Guidelines:
   • Eat a variety of foods
   • Maintain a healthy weight
   • Choose a diet low in fat, saturated fat, and cholesterol
   • Choose a diet with plenty of vegetables, fruits, and grain products
   • Use sugars only in moderation
   • Use salt and sodium only in moderation
   • If you drink alcoholic beverages, do so in moderation
4. Use the principles of balance, variety and moderation, and read food labels.
5. habits, customs, and beliefs about food in a particular culture
6. *Mediterranean:* the diet includes seafood, meat, cheese, fruits, and vegetables; most of the fat comes from olive oil; people consider the diet to be a heart-healthy diet
   Chinese: the diet includes rice, meat, seafood, poultry and eggs mixed with vegetables, soups and tea; it's low in fat and high in fiber; it's a good diet when salt is reduced

B. Reviewing Ideas

○ Go over the directions.
○ Have students work with a partner to read and revise their previous answers. See instructions and answer key for Activity B on page 130.

C. Discussion

○ Go over the directions and the questions.
○ Have students discuss the questions in small groups.
○ Call on students to share their ideas with the class.

ANSWER KEY

Answers will vary.

CRITICAL THINKING STRATEGY: Comparing Sources of Information

○ Go over the information in the box.
○ Ask questions: *What are* theories? *How should you look for information if there are different opinions on a subject?*

D. Making Connections: Comparing Sources of Information

○ Go over the directions and the questions.
○ Have students discuss the questions in pairs.
○ Call on students to share their ideas with the class.

ANSWER KEY

Answers may vary.
1. Most of the information is similar, but the lecture includes seafood.
2. The Mediterranean diet is high in the kind of fat that does not raise "bad" cholesterol which leads to heart disease.

E. Comparing Source Information

○ Go over the directions.
○ Have students do Internet research on the Mediterranean diet. Remind students to use the tips in the directions.
○ Call on students to tell the class something new they found out.

Put It All Together

A. Taking a Survey

○ Go over the information about the group project at the top of page 138.
○ Have students interview four classmates and record their answers in the chart.

SPEAKING STRATEGY: Taking Turns

○ Go over the information in the box.
○ Ask questions: *What does* collaborate *mean? How can you get quieter group members to talk? What can help you speak up if you are shy?*

B. Creating a Meal Plan

○ Go over the directions and the steps.
Step 1
○ Have students work in small groups to create a meal with dishes from each of the five groups. Remind students to use the survey results.
○ Direct students' attention to the meal plan on page 140. Have students write their ideas there.
Step 2
○ Go over the directions and the sources for information on nutrients.
○ Have students work in groups to find out and list the nutrients for each dish on their menus.
○ Have students finalize their menus after analyzing the nutrient information for the dishes.

C. Discussing Meal Plans

○ Go over the directions.
○ Have students present their menus to the class. For a variation on the presentation, see the Expansion Activity that follows.
○ Have the class vote on the best menu and give reasons for their votes.

EXPANSION ACTIVITY: Menu Gallery

○ Divide each group from Activity C into subgroups A and B.
○ Post the menus on the walls around the room.
○ Have students in Subgroup A stay by their menus and explain the dishes and nutrient content. Have the students in Subgroup B circulate, asking questions about each menu.
○ Set a time limit of 10 minutes, then have students exchange roles.
○ Again set a time limit of 10 minutes.
○ Have students vote on the best menu.

Unit 2 Vocabulary Workshop

A. Matching
○ Go over the directions.
○ Have students write the correct letters on the lines
  to match the definitions with the words.
○ Go over the answers.

ANSWER KEY
1. g; 2. c; 3. j; 4. b; 5. a; 6. f; 7. i; 8. d; 9. h; 10. e

B. Sentence Halves
○ Go over the directions.
○ Have students write the correct letters on the lines
  to match the two halves of each sentence.
○ Go over the answers.

ANSWER KEY
1. c; 2. a; 3. e; 4. b; 5. d

C. High Frequency Words
○ Go over the directions.
○ Have students write the correct words on the lines.
○ Go over the answers.

ANSWER KEY
1. park; 2. female; 3. baby; 4. curled; 5. hunt;
6. hungry; 7. asleep; 8. terrible; 9. hit; 10. swept;
11. ocean; 12. male

Unit Opener, page 143

❍ Direct students' attention to the photo and the unit and chapter titles on page 143.
❍ Brainstorm ideas for what the unit will include and write students' ideas on the board.

CHAPTER 5 THE DAYS OF SLAVERY

In Part 1, students will read a passage about African Americans and slavery. In Part 2, students will listen to a student and professor talking about the antislavery movement in U.S. history. In Part 4, students will read about and listen to a radio program on a type of music known as spirituals. In Part 5, students will listen to a lecture about the Underground Railroad. Finally, students will do a group presentation on an historical movement.

VOCABULARY

affirming	conductor	enslaved	Rainbow Coalition	speak out against
analyze	crops	find their way	raised funds	stop by
arrested	denounced	first-hand	rebellion	stop in
bump into	depended	held public office	regions	supported
came into existence	dimension	maximum distance	resources	survived
caption	drop by	meet up with	role	vivid
chronological	drop in on	motivated to	role model	well laid-out
code	economy	network	run into	win freedom
colony	enduring	perseverance	significant	

LISTENING STRATEGIES

Being Prepared for an Important Explanation
Listening for Examples in Groups
Listening for Dates

CRITICAL THINKING STRATEGIES

Using a Timeline (Part 2)
Listening to Feedback (Part 5)
Note: Strategy in bold is highlighted in the Student Book.

MECHANICS OF LISTENING AND SPEAKING

Language Functions: Introducing Yourself to Someone
   Who Doesn't Remember You
   Responding to an Introduction
   Identifying Yourself on the Telephone
Pronunciation: /I/ vs. /i/
Words in Phrases: Verb Phrases for Meeting People

SPEAKING STRATEGIES

Working Cooperatively
Getting and Giving Feedback

TEST-TAKING STRATEGY

Previewing: Brainstorming Possible Vocabulary

CHAPTER 5   The Days of Slavery

Chapter 5 Opener, page 145

- ○ Direct students' attention to the photo and chapter title. Go over the directions and questions.
- ○ Put students in pairs to share their ideas.
- ○ Call on students to share their ideas with the class.

PART ① INTRODUCTION
AFRICAN AMERICANS AND SLAVERY, PAGES 146–150

A. Using Pictures

- ○ Direct students' attention to the photos. Ask a comprehension question: *What do you see?*
- ○ Go over the directions and the questions.
- ○ Put students in pairs to discuss the questions.
- ○ Call on students to share their ideas with the class.

ANSWER KEY
Answers will vary but should include the ideas in the captions on page 146.

EXPANSION ACTIVITY: Captions

- ○ Bring to class some news photos and captions from magazines or newspapers, or assign students to bring some in.
- ○ Cut the captions off the photos.
- ○ Put students in pairs or small groups. Give each group several photos.
- ○ Have students write captions for the photos.
- ○ Have students match the original captions with the photos and compare their captions with the originals.

B. Thinking Ahead

- ○ Go over the directions and the questions.
- ○ Put students in small groups to discuss the questions.
- ○ Call on students to share their ideas with the class.

C. Reading

- ○ Go over the directions and the questions.
- ○ Direct students' attention to the visuals and captions and ask: *What can you tell about slavery from the art?*
- ○ Have students read the passage and discuss the question in pairs or small groups.

Culture Notes

- ○ Historically, slavery has existed in most parts of the world. After the Americas were colonized by European countries, slavery flourished in Brazil, the Caribbean, and the United States.
- ○ In English, *north, south, east,* and *west* are not capitalized when they mean directions, but they are capitalized when they refer to specific places. In this chapter, *the North* and *the South* refer to the parts of the U.S. that fought in the Civil War. Today, *the South* still refers to the region where slavery existed, but *the North* is no longer a common phrase.

CRITICAL THINKING STRATEGY: Using a Timeline

- ○ Go over the information in the box.
- ○ Ask comprehension questions: *What does a timeline show? How is it helpful?*

TOEFL® iBT Tip

TOEFL iBT Tip 1: In the fit and explain and the general/specific tasks on the TOEFL iBT, examinees will have to synthesize information from both a text and a spoken source.

- ○ Point out that being able to read and interpret a reading text will be helpful in building up to the integrated speaking task.

- ○ The critical thinking strategy *Using a Timeline* will help students to organize their thoughts for the speaking task by creating a logical graphic organizer for a reading.

D. Using a Timeline

○ Go over the directions.
○ Have students complete the timeline and compare timelines with a partner.
○ Go over the answers with the class. You may want to copy the timeline on the board and ask for volunteers to fill in the information.

Academic Notes

○ You may want to point out that some timelines only show the order of events, like the one in Activity D. More often, timelines also show the length of time between events.
○ When you copy the timeline on the board in Activity D to show the answers, you may want to illustrate the length of time by leaving a wider space for longer gaps in time.

ANSWER KEY

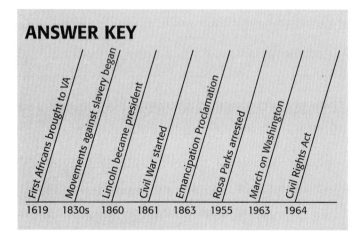

| 1619 | 1830s | 1860 | 1861 | 1863 | 1955 | 1963 | 1964 |

E. Vocabulary Check

○ Go over the directions.
○ Have students write the words or phrases on the lines and then compare answers with a partner.
○ Go over the answers with the class.

ANSWER KEY

1. colony; 2. survived; 3. economy; 4. crops;
5. enslaved; 6. depended on; 7. rebellion; 8. arrested;
9. held public office

Vocabulary Notes

○ The passage contains many words with prefixes and suffixes. In general, prefixes change the meaning of the base word somewhat, while suffixes often change the part of speech.
○ Prefixes in the passage include: *en–, in–, il–, un–,* and *pro–.* Suffixes include: *–ed/–en, –ly, –ation, –ern, –ion, –ent, –ers, –ment, –ist, –ery, –hood, –ity,* and *–ous.*

EXPANSION ACTIVITY: Word Families

○ Model the activity. Write one of the words from the passage with a prefix or a suffix (e.g., *enslaved*) on the board. Underline the base word (e.g., *slave*). Elicit the part of speech (noun). Elicit other words with the same base (*slavery, slavish*).
○ Have students work in pairs to find examples of each of the prefixes and suffixes mentioned in the Vocabulary Notes.
○ Have students underline the base word in each example they find. Point out that sometimes the base word is slightly different from how it appears in the word with a prefix or suffix.
○ Instruct students to write the base word in parentheses if it is spelled differently with a prefix or suffix.
○ Have students list as many words as possible with the same base word.

ANSWER KEY

Examples of words in passage: en<u>slave</u>d, <u>independen</u>t, <u>il</u>legal, un<u>fair</u>, proclamation (<u>claim</u>), <u>indenture</u>d, <u>main</u>ly, <u>plantation</u>, <u>southern</u>, permission (<u>permit</u>), <u>Northern</u>ers, <u>treatment</u>, abolitionist (<u>abolish</u>), <u>slavery</u>, <u>neighbor</u>hood, <u>equal</u>ity, religious (<u>religion</u>)

F. Discussion

○ Go over the directions and the questions.
○ Have students discuss the questions in small groups.
○ Call on students to share their ideas with the class.

ANSWER KEY

Answers will vary.

G. Journal Writing

❍ Go over the directions.
❍ Explain that this is a freewriting activity and does not have to be perfect. Point out that journal writing can be a warm-up to a more structured writing assignment, helping to generate ideas.
❍ Set a time limit of 10 minutes.
❍ Put students in pairs to read or talk about their writing.

PART ② SOCIAL LANGUAGE
ABOUT THAT ASSIGNMENT, PAGES 151–154

Before Listening
A. Thinking Ahead

❍ Go over the directions and the steps.
❍ Divide the class into two groups, A and B.
❍ Have students read the appropriate paragraph.
❍ Pair each student from Group A with a student from Group B.
❍ Have students work in pairs, taking turns asking and answering the questions in their box.
❍ Go over the answers with the class.

ANSWER KEY

Answers to Group A's questions:
1. Many Southern whites hated abolitionists.
2. Southerners believed slavery was necessary for the economy, and that slavery existed in many societies in the past.
3. The difference between the North and South about slavery

Answers to Group B's questions:
1. Some Northerners were against slavery, but not all.
2. Most Northerners discriminated against blacks.
3. Abolitionists wanted all slavery to end.

EXPANSION ACTIVITY: Role Play

❍ Write on the board *1. Abolitionist 2. Free Black 3. Non-abolitionist Northerner 4. Southerner.*
❍ Explain that students will pretend to be a member of one of these groups.
❍ Divide the class into four groups without letting students know what group other students are in. You can have students draw numbers, or just whisper each student's group to them.
❍ Have students stand and walk around the room to talk to classmates. Have students ask each other questions about their opinions about slavery. Remind them to answer not with their own opinions, but with the opinions of their group.
❍ Have students write their guesses of each student's group on a piece of paper.
❍ As a class, go over who was in which group and how other students knew.

B. Vocabulary Preparation

❍ Go over the directions.
❍ Have students match the definitions with the words in red.
❍ Go over the answers with the class.

ANSWER KEY

1. a; 2. d; 3. b; 4. c; 5. e

Listening
A. Listening for the Main Idea

❍ Direct students' attention to the photo.
❍ Go over the directions and the question.
❍ Play the video or audio program.
❍ Ask students: *Why is Chrissy talking to the professor?*

Audio Script

Chrissy: Uh, excuse me, Dr. Taylor?
Dr. Taylor: Hi, you're, uh . . .
Chrissy: Chrissy. I'm in your American History class.
Dr. Taylor: Right, Chrissy. Have a seat.
Chrissy: Thanks.
Dr. Taylor: What can I do for you?
Chrissy: Uh, it's about the assignment for next week.

Dr. Taylor: Mm-hm.

Chrissy: Unfortunately, I had to leave class about 10 minutes early yesterday, so I didn't get the assignment. What exactly are we supposed to write about?

Dr. Taylor: Well, you're supposed to analyze the social issues that led to the rise of the antislavery movement of the early 1800s.

Chrissy: Gee, was that in the lecture?

Dr. Taylor: No, but have you read Chapter 3 yet?

Chrissy: Well, no, not yet.

Dr. Taylor: Well, that's all you have to do. It's very well laid out in that chapter. You need to look at the regions these people represented, and their role in society. For example, there were the New England abolitionists.

Chrissy: Oh, yeah, the poets, uh, James Russell Lowell and John Greenleaf Whittier.

Dr. Taylor: Right. What was their reason for supporting the abolition of slavery?

Chrissy: Right.

Dr. Taylor: And the whole role of women in the movement—Lucretia Mott and the Grimké sisters. You need to look at the role of women in American society at the time to explain what might have motivated women of that particular social class to participate in the movement.

Chrissy: Yeah, I see.

Dr. Taylor: And don't forget to mention the role of the free blacks who were involved.

Chrissy: Oh, yeah, like Frederick Douglass and Sojourner Truth.

Dr. Taylor: Right. So, you've got these three different— *[phone rings]* Excuse me. *[to the person on the phone]* Hello? Oh, hi, Dr. Dorwick. No, um, could you hold for a moment please? *[to Chrissy]* I'm sorry, Chrissy, I'm going to have to take this call.

Chrissy: Oh, that's OK. I think I understand what to do.

Dr. Taylor: Great!

Chrissy: Thanks so much. I really appreciate it.

Dr. Taylor: You're welcome.

Chrissy: Thanks again. Bye.

Dr. Taylor: Bye, bye. See you tomorrow . . . Hi.

ANSWER KEY

Chrissy is talking to the professor to find out about the assignment.

B. Listening For Details

○ Go over the directions.
○ Have students read the questions. Point out that reading the questions first helps them to know what to listen for.
○ Have students answer the questions as you play the video or audio program.
○ Repeat if necessary.
○ Have students compare answers with a partner.
○ Go over the answers with the class.

TOEFL® iBT Tip

TOEFL iBT Tip 2: The TOEFL iBT measures the ability to understand the main idea and important details of a conversation or a lecture.

○ Point out that the *Listening for Main Ideas* and *Listening for Details* activities help students improve their overall basic comprehension skills.

○ On the TOEFL iBT, main idea questions may appear in the following formats:
   What are the speakers mainly discussing?
   Why does the student want to talk to his professor?

Audio Script

Chrissy: Uh, excuse me, Dr. Taylor?

Dr. Taylor: Hi, you're, uh . . .

Chrissy: Chrissy. I'm in your American History class.

Dr. Taylor: Right, Chrissy. Have a seat.

Chrissy: Thanks.

Dr. Taylor: What can I do for you?

Chrissy: Uh, it's about the assignment for next week.

Dr. Taylor: Mm-hm.

Chrissy: Unfortunately, I had to leave class about 10 minutes early yesterday, so I didn't get the assignment. What exactly are we supposed to write about?

Dr. Taylor: Well, you're supposed to analyze the social issues that led to the rise of the antislavery movement of the early 1800s.

Chrissy: Gee, was that in the lecture?

Dr. Taylor: No, but have you read Chapter 3 yet?

Chrissy: Well, no, not yet.

> **Dr. Taylor:** Well, that's all you have to do. It's very well laid out in that chapter.

ANSWER KEY
1. American History; 2. She had to leave 10 minutes early. 3. the early 1800s. 4. in Chapter 3

 C. Listening for Categories
- Go over the directions.
- Have students write the three groups of abolitionists as you play the video or audio program.
- Have students compare answers with a partner.
- Go over the answers with the class.

Audio Script
Dr. Taylor: Well, you're supposed to analyze the social issues that led to the rise of the antislavery movement of the early 1800s.
Chrissy: Gee, was that in the lecture?
Dr. Taylor: No, but have you read Chapter 3 yet?
Chrissy: Well, no, not yet.
Dr. Taylor: Well that's all you have to do. It's very well laid out in that chapter. You need to look at the regions these people represented, and their role in society. For example, there were the New England abolitionists.
Chrissy: Oh, yeah, the poets, ah, James Russell Lowell and John Greenleaf Whittier.
Dr. Taylor: Right. What was their reason for supporting the abolition of slavery?
Chrissy: Oh, right.
Dr. Taylor: And the whole role of women in the movement—Lucretia Mott and the Grimké sisters. You need to look at the role of women in American society at the time to explain what might have motivated women of that particular social class to participate in the movement.
Chrissy: Yeah, I see.
Dr. Taylor: And don't forget to mention the role of the free blacks who were involved.
Chrissy: Oh, yeah, like Frederick Douglass and Sojourner Truth.
Dr. Taylor: Right. So, you've got these three different—
[phone rings]

ANSWER KEY
1. the poets; 2. the women; 3. the free blacks

 EXPANSION ACTIVITY: Online Research Groups
- Have students do Internet research on one of the people mentioned in Activity C (Lowell, Whittier, Mott, Grimké sisters, Douglass, or Truth).
- Have students get in groups according to who they researched and share information.
- Have the groups create three questions about important facts about the person researched.
- Collect the questions.
- Recombine groups so that each group includes one student representing each research topic.
- Have students tell group members about their researched person. Explain that students will take a quiz on all the research topics and everyone in the group will receive the grade of the students with the lowest score.
- Read the collected questions aloud and have students work individually to answer the questions on paper.
- Correct the "quizzes" with the class.

After Listening

A. Information Gap

○ Go over the directions and the questions.
○ Put students in pairs. Have Student A in each pair turn to page 204 and Student B turn to page 208.
○ Have students complete the charts and then check their answers with their partner.
○ Go over the answers with the class.

ANSWER KEY

Free Blacks	Women	New England Poets
Frederick Douglass	Lucretia Mott	John Greenleaf Whittier
Sojourner Truth	the Grimké sisters	James Russell Lowell

B. Discussion

○ Go over the directions and the questions.
○ Have students discuss the questions in pairs.
○ Call on students to share their ideas with the class.

ANSWER KEY

Answers will vary.

PART ③ THE MECHANICS OF LISTENING AND SPEAKING, PAGES 154–159

LANGUAGE FUNCTIONS: Introducing Yourself to Someone Who Doesn't Remember You

○ Go over the information in the box.
○ Ask: *What are some ways you can introduce yourself to someone who doesn't remember you?*

Responding to an Introduction

○ Go over the information in the box.
○ Ask: *What are some ways you can respond when someone you don't remember introduces himself or herself to you?*

🎧 A. Listening to Introductions

○ Go over the directions.
○ Have students write the words and expressions they hear as you play the audio program.
○ Go over the answers with the class.

Audio Script

1. **A:** Hi, I'm John. I'm in your English class.
   B: Oh, yeah, sure. Hi, John.
2. **A:** Hello. You may not recognize me. My name is John.
   B: Oh, yes, hello, John.
3. **A:** Hi. I'm John Martinez. We met last week.
   B: Hi, John. Nice to see you again.
4. **A:** Hi. I'm John.
   B: Hi, John. How have you been?
5. **A:** Hi, I'm John. I'm in your English class.
   B: I'm sorry. I didn't recognize you at first.

ANSWER KEY

1. in your English class; 2. may not recognize me; 3. Nice to see you again; 4. Hi, John. How have you been? 5. I didn't recognize you at first.

B. Introducing Yourself

○ Go over the directions.
○ Put students in pairs, with one partner playing the role of Student A and the other Student B.
○ Have students take turns introducing themselves and responding appropriately.
○ Walk around the room to monitor the activity and provide help as needed.
○ Have volunteers role play their conversations in front of the class.

Identifying Yourself on the Telephone
- ❍ Go over the information in the box.
- ❍ Ask questions: *What does* identify yourself *mean? What are some informal ways to identify yourself? What is a more formal way?* (The third example is more formal.)

C. Identifying Yourself on the Telephone
- ❍ Go over the directions.
- ❍ Have students write the words or expressions they hear as you play the audio program.
- ❍ Put students in pairs to compare answers.
- ❍ Go over the answers with the class.

Audio Script
1. **A:** Hello?
   B: Hi. It's Dawn Wu. Is this Jim?
   A: Oh, hi, Dawn.
2. **A:** Hello?
   B: Hi, Jim. It's Dawn.
   A: Oh, hi, Dawn.
3. **A:** Hello?
   B: Hello. This is Dawn Wu.
   A: Hello, Dawn.

ANSWER KEY
1. Hello; Oh, hi, Dawn; 2. It's Dawn; 3. This is Dawn Wu; Hello

PRONUNCIATION: /I/ vs. /i/
- ❍ Go over the information in the box. Play the audio program.
- ❍ Ask comprehension questions: *Which sound is longer? What position is your mouth in when you make the /i/ sound?*

Pronunciation Note
- ❍ You may want to point out that the /i/ sound is longer and that your mouth is wider side to side, almost in a smile when you make this sound. The /I/ sound is a little shorter, and you don't need to stretch your mouth at all.

D. Hearing the Difference Between /I/ and /i/
- ❍ Go over the directions.
- ❍ Have students circle the words they hear as you play the audio program.
- ❍ Go over the answers with the class.
- ❍ Play the audio program again and have students repeat the words.

Audio Script
1. bit	6. seat
2. bin	7. eat
3. pick	8. live
4. his	9. dip
5. peak	10. meat

ANSWER KEY
1. bit; 2. bin; 3. pick; 4. his; 5. peak; 6. seat; 7. eat; 8. live; 9. dip; 10. meat

EXPANSION ACTIVITY: Pronunciation Bingo
- ❍ Have students create 4 x 4 grids for a Bingo game.
- ❍ Ask students to choose 16 of the words in Exercise D and write one in each of the squares of the Bingo grid.
- ❍ Have students call out *Bingo* when they have filled four squares in a row.
- ❍ Call out words in random order from Exercise D and have students mark off the words they hear on their grids.
- ❍ When a student calls out *Bingo,* have the student read out each of the words in the line for the class to check.
- ❍ Repeat the game a few more times.
- ❍ In a variation, put students in pairs to take turns saying and marking off the words on their grids.

E. Pronouncing /I/ and /i/
- ❍ Go over the directions.
- ❍ Put students in pairs to take turns saying and underlining the words in Activity D.

EXPANSION ACTIVITY: What Did You Say?

○ Write the following questions on the board:
Why did you live/leave there?
Do you want to pick/peek?
What size are your bins/beans?
Where did you put the mitt/meat?

○ Elicit appropriate responses for each question. For example, an answer to *Why did you live there?* might be *My parents moved there when I was three.* An answer to *Why did you leave there?* might be *I wanted to go to school in the United States.*

○ Model the activity. Call on a student and ask: *Where did you put the mitt?* Elicit an appropriate answer (e.g., *in the closet, but not in the refrigerator*).

○ Have students take turns to practice saying the sentences and responding appropriately.

F. Pronouncing /I/ and /i/ in Conversations

○ Go over the directions.

○ Direct students' attention to the chart. Go over the questions.

○ Have students talk to their classmates to ask and answer the questions. Remind students to write the names of their classmates on the chart.

WORDS IN PHRASES: Verb Phrases for Meeting People

○ Go over the information in the box.

○ Ask comprehension questions: *What parts of speech are in these verb phrases? What is an expression that means* to meet unexpectedly? *What is an expression that means* to visit?

TOEFL® iBT Tip

TOEFL iBT Tip 3: In the lectures and conversations on the TOEFL iBT, students will hear speech that is realistic and natural in English and includes reductions.

○ Point out that the *Verb Phrases for Meeting People* activity will help students distinguish these phrases in campus conversations.

○ Students will also need to produce *intelligible* speech and effectively use colloquial phrases in order to succeed on the speaking part of the test.

Put It Together

Introducing Yourself

○ Go over the directions.

○ Put students in pairs. Have one student in each pair be Student A and the other Student B.

○ Have students act out the situations.

○ Walk around to monitor the activity and provide help as needed.

○ Call on volunteers to act out the situations in front of the class.

PART BROADCAST ENGLISH
MUSIC OF THE UNDERGROUND RAILROAD, PAGES 160–164

Before Listening

TEST-TAKING STRATEGY: Previewing: Brainstorming Possible Vocabulary

○ Go over the information in the box.

○ Ask: *What is one way to prepare for listening to a topic you know something about?*

A. Brainstorming Possible Vocabulary

○ Go over the directions.

○ Have students discuss the questions in pairs.

○ Call on students to share their ideas with the class.

ANSWER KEY

1. trains; 2. takes tickets, helps passengers; 3. to go under mountains, cities, and water

B. Background Reading

○ Go over the directions.

○ Have students read the passage.

C. Comprehension Check
- ○ Go over the directions and the questions.
- ○ Have students discuss the questions in small groups.
- ○ Call on students to share their ideas with the class.

ANSWER KEY
1. Spirituals are faith songs that are part of the folk tradition of African Americans; 2. to express religious beliefs, to express slaves' wish for freedom and escape, to send secret messages about escaping

D. Vocabulary Preparation
- ○ Go over the directions.
- ○ Have students match the definitions in the box with the words and phrases in red and then compare answers with a partner.
- ○ Go over the answers with the class.

ANSWER KEY
1. b; 2. c; 3. e; 4. a; 5. f; 6. d

EXPANSION ACTIVITY: Beanbag Toss
- ○ Tell students they have one minute to review the vocabulary from Activity D.
- ○ After one minute, ask students to close their books.
- ○ Tell students that you will call on a student and toss a beanbag or ball. You will say one of the definitions, and the students should respond with the vocabulary word or phrase and throw the beanbag back.
- ○ Call on a student and toss the beanbag, saying *strong or clear.* Elicit an answer from the student (*vivid*) and have them toss the beanbag or ball back to you.
- ○ Repeat with other students. This is a fast-paced activity.

Listening
🎧 A. Listening for the Main Idea: Section 1
- ○ Go over the directions.
- ○ Have students write the answer to the question as you play the audio program.
- ○ Go over the answer with the students.

Audio Script
Kim and Reggie (singing):
No more ox and blood for me
No more no more
No more ox and blood for me
Many thousand gone
No more pickin' corn for me
No more no more
No more pickin' corn for me
Many thousand gone…

Host: Kim and Reggie Harris have been singing and telling stories for nearly 20 years now. They met each other at summer camp in 1974, married in 1976, and began touring together in 1980. It was then they were asked to do a presentation at a school assembly. They decided that the Underground Railroad would be their subject.

Their first recording on that subject was called "Music of the Underground Railroad." Their second recording, following it, is called, "Steal Away: Songs of the Underground Railroad." Kim and Reggie Harris join us from the studios of Peachstate Public Radio. Welcome, both of you.

Kim: Thank you.

Reggie: Oh, thank you. It's great to be here.

Host: For those who might not know or remember what the Underground Railroad was, give us a brief explanation.

Kim: The Underground Railroad really was people who were working very hard in the cause of freedom during the days of slavery. Uh, it was really run by the free African-American community, which makes a lot of sense since they had a lot to gain from helping their family and friends and people get out of slavery. But they also had help from people of different races who believed in freedom. So we love to say the Underground Railroad was America's first Rainbow Coalition.

Host: Ah, it was not a train—it was people.

Kim: It was people.

Reggie: It was not a train. And we often say that, uh, in our performances, because, uh, you can talk about the Underground Railroad and the fact that it was people, and the enduring image is people digging tunnels, or, uh, taking a train to freedom. And, uh, so part of what we do is to dispel that myth.

Host: One of the things you like to say is that you like to sing songs of heroes and "sheroes." One of the sheroes you devote a song to on your new CD is Harriet Tubman. Now she was one of the main "conductors" on this railroad.

Reggie: She was, and, you know, Harriet Tubman is just such a fascinating character. A woman, you know, a black woman in the 1800s, uh, she couldn't read, she couldn't write, she had very few resources, if any. And she has become an enduring historical figure. We like to particularly tell young people that here is a great role model of someone who had very little going for her, and, and yet managed through sheer perseverance and determination and the love of her people to do something so great, that we're still talking about her today.

ANSWER KEY

They sing songs about the Underground Railroad.

LISTENING STRATEGY: Being Prepared for an Important Explanation

○ Go over the information in the box.
○ Ask questions: *Do interviewers always let you know an important explanation is coming? When they do, what expressions should you notice?*

TOEFL® iBT Tip

TOEFL iBT Tip 4: independent and integrated speaking tasks may require examinees to support an opinion about a topic with reasons and explanations. Students may also hear a conversation and be asked to express and support an opinion of what they heard.

○ Point out that the listening strategy *Being Prepared for an Important Explanation* will help students learn the "chunks" of language that are used as sentence starters to introduce an explanation.

○ Learning these phrases and how to use them will also help students to respond more succinctly and completely to the speaking task.

🎧 B. Being Prepared for an Important Explanation

○ Go over the directions.
○ Have students answer the question as you play the audio program and then compare answers with a partner.
○ Go over the answer with the class.

Audio Script

○ Use the Listening Script for Activity A on page 93 of the Teacher's Edition.

ANSWER KEY

people who were working very hard in the cause of freedom during the days of slavery, helping people get out of slavery

🎧 C. Guessing the Meaning from Context

○ Go over the directions.
○ Have students fill in the correct bubble as you play the audio program.
○ Go over the answers with the class.

Audio Script

1. One of the things you like to say is that you like to sing songs of heroes and "sheroes." One of the sheroes you devote a song to on your new CD is Harriet Tubman. Now she was one of the main "conductors" on the railroad.

2. She was, and you know, Harriet Tubman is just such a fascinating character. A woman, you know, a black woman in the 1800s—she couldn't read, she couldn't write, she had very few resources, if any. And she has become an enduring historical figure.

3. We like to particularly tell young people that here is a great role model of someone who had very little going for her, and, and yet managed through sheer perseverance and determination and the love of her people to do something so great, that we're still talking about her today.

4. They were songs that were used as code songs. Uh, they were used as mapping songs. People could take a song like "Wade in the Water" and remember that you need to stay near water.

ANSWER KEY
1. B; 2. C; 3. A; 4. B

TOEFL® iBT Tip

TOEFL iBT Tip 5: Understanding vocabulary in the context of a conversation or lecture is an integral part of the listening comprehension section of the TOEFL iBT.

○ Point out that the activity *Guessing the Meaning from Context* will help students to identify words or terms that are new or unfamiliar by helping them focus on language that they already know.

○ Mention that when new vocabulary phrases are formed from more common words, students can often guess the meaning of the phrase from the meaning of individual words.

D. Listening to a Description
○ Go over the directions and the question.
○ Have students write the answer as you play the audio program.
○ Have students compare ideas with a partner.
○ Go over the answers with the class.

Audio Script
Host: One of the things you like to say is that you like to sing songs of heroes and "sheroes." One of the sheroes you devote a song to on your new CD is Harriet Tubman. Now she was one of the main "conductors" on this railroad.

Reggie: She was, and, you know, Harriet Tubman is just such a fascinating character. A woman, you know, a black woman in the 1800s, uh, she couldn't read, she couldn't write, she had very few resources, if any. And she has become an enduring historical figure. We like to particularly tell young people that here is a great role model of someone who had very little going for her, and, and yet managed through sheer perseverance and determination and the love of her people to do something so great, that we're still talking about her today.

ANSWER KEY
Answers may vary.
Harriet Tubman was fascinating, a black woman who couldn't read or write but became a historical figure. She was a great role model, had perseverance and determination and the love of her people.

EXPANSION ACTIVITY: Describing a Person
○ Elicit ideas about the kinds of information that can go in a description of a person (e.g., *gender, physical description, rich or poor, occupation, personal qualities*).
○ Have students write a description of the person they researched in the "Online Research Groups" activity on page 89 of the Teacher's Edition.
○ Have students read their descriptions aloud. Elicit the name of the person from the class.

E. Listening for Examples: Section 2
○ Go over the directions and the questions.
○ Have students answer the questions as you play the audio program.
○ Have students compare their answers in small groups.
○ Go over the answers with the class.

Audio Script

Host: What was the significance of the music?

Reggie: The music was significant in that, first of all, it, it brought hope. Ah, the songs are—are songs of faith, and they are songs that, that, uh, gave people great hope, uh, in that faith. And yet, they were very practical songs as well. They were songs that were used as code songs, uh—they were used as mapping songs. People could take a song like "Wade in the Water," and remember that you needed to stay near water. Not only because you needed water to drink, but also because fish live in the water. So you could, on your escape, have something to eat. Uh, animals coming down to the water to drink, you might be able to catch one. Uh, essentially, you also needed to remember that you needed to wade in the water—you needed to walk through water whenever you could to kill your scent and so that you didn't leave tracks.

So they were, were songs with sort of two realities going on, uh, faith and, and keeping people, uh focused on the fact that they wanted to get to freedom, but also providing them the tools to do exactly that.

Kim and Reggie (singing):
Wade in the water
Wade in the water, children,
Wade in the water
God's gonna trouble the water
Ooh, those children all dressed in white
God's gonna trouble the water
Must be the waters, get ready to fly
God's gonna trouble the water
Wade in the water

Host: Where would slaves have had the opportunity to, to sing a song like "Wade in the Water" to pass along that information without getting caught?

Kim: Well at times you could sing it, uh, while the master or the overseer was listening because they were faith songs. And many of the slaves were being encouraged to take up Christianity as their religion, and so at times you could sing it right when the master was listening. Other times you might just sing it at a secret meeting, or hum it to yourself to remind yourself and to remind others of these, uh, tools for freedom.

Host: There's a beautiful song. It's called "Steal Away." How is "Steal Away" connected to Harriet Tubman?

Kim: It was one of the songs that, that people like Harriet Tubman and also others who were preparing to escape could sing the night before they were leaving as a signal to let other people know that they would be going. And I guess there is an anecdote that says that she sang that song right walking past her master. She was humming and singing to herself:

Steal away to Jesus
Steal away home
I ain't got long to stay here…

And the anecdote says that he just, you know, nodded to her. She nodded to him and he didn't get it that she was going to be leaving soon.

Host: Huh.

Reggie: It was often believed that a singing slave was a happy slave. So many masters just sort of felt like if they were singing songs and singing in particular about going to heaven, or singing about God, then they were just happy and, uh, happy with their faith, so they left them alone.

Kim and Reggie (singing):
Steal away
Steal away home
I ain't got long to stay
I ain't got long to stay . . .

Host: These songs are still sung at religious gatherings, at community gatherings, civic gatherings around the country. Why are they still so popular?

Reggie: Part of it is their, their great power and their great beauty. I mean, they are truly wonderful songs. They are, in many ways, so—so very affirming to sing. And, uh, and they have remained part of the, uh, community of faith. I grew—you know, I grew up singing these songs. I remember vivid memories of "Wade in the Water" at my church, uh, during baptism. And, uh, the choir just singing, and, and—which is sort of being taken almost to another place, listening to the words, uh, not even realizing at that time that it—that song in particular had a whole 'nother dimension to it.

ANSWER KEY

1. It told the slaves to stay near water for something to drink and eat, and to wade in the water so they could kill their scent and didn't leave tracks.
2. They were Christian faith songs and many slaves were encouraged to take up Christianity.
3. The master thought the song was about going to heaven, but it was really about escaping.

Culture Note

○ When slaves escaped, their owners often sent teams of men and dogs to recapture them before they reached freedom in the North. The dogs would track the slaves by scent, so wading in the water could confuse the dogs and allow the slaves to escape.

After Listening

A. Discussion

○ Go over the directions and the questions.
○ Put students in small groups to discuss the questions.
○ Call on students to share their ideas with the class.

ANSWER KEY

Answers will vary.

B. Applying Information

○ Go over the directions.
○ Have students discuss the question in pairs.
○ Call on students to share their ideas with the class.

ANSWER KEY

The "drinking gourd" is a code for the constellation Ursa Major, or the Big Dipper. The song is telling slaves to follow the river and then the Big Dipper to another river.

Culture Note

○ Make sure students understand the connection between the constellation the Big Dipper and the drinking gourd in the song. Both are long-handled ladles. A dipper or drinking gourd would be used by a group of workers, such as the slaves, when drinking out of a common water source, like a bucket.

PART ⑤ ACADEMIC ENGLISH
THE UNDERGROUND RAILROAD, PAGES 164–173

Before Listening

A. Thinking Ahead

○ Direct students' attention to the picture of the routes of the Underground Railroad. Ask questions: *Where did the Underground Railroad go? What states did it pass through?*
○ Go over the directions and the questions.
○ Have students discuss the questions in small groups.
○ Call on students to share their ideas with the class.

ANSWER KEY

Answers will vary.
It would be best to escape at night when it's dark and you wouldn't be missed from work.
You could get food from the kitchen or from the fields. Other slaves and abolitionists might help you escape. You might feel excited and afraid.

B. Vocabulary Preparation

○ Go over the directions.
○ Have students complete the sentences with words or phrases from the box and then compare answers with a partner.
○ Go over the answers with the class.

ANSWER KEY

1. raised funds; 2. denounced; 3. first-hand;
4. the maximum distance; 5. network; 6. supported;
7. significant

EXPANSION ACTIVITY: Original Sentences
○ Have students write original sentences using the vocabulary words.
○ Put students in pairs to compare sentences.
○ Call on students to read their sentences to the class.

C. Vocabulary Preparation: Words in Phrases

○ Go over the directions and the vocabulary words.
○ Have students match the definitions to the verb phrases in red.
○ Go over the answers with the class.

ANSWER KEY

1. b; 2. a; 3. d; 4. c

Listening

 A. Guessing the Meaning From Context

○ Go over the directions.
○ Have students fill in the correct bubbles as you play the audio or video program.
○ Have students compare answers with a partner.
○ Go over the answers with the class.

Audio Script

1. A number of former slaves, such as Frederick Douglass, Harriet Tubman, and Sojourner Truth, supported the Underground Railroad movement. Uh, you read about them in Chapter 23—right? That's Frederick Douglass, Harriet Tubman, and Sojourner Truth. They were well known for speaking out against slavery, and uh, Tubman became one of the most famous conductors of the railroad. By "conductor," I mean that she actually helped the slaves on their journey of escape from the South to the North.

2. Another group organized in the antislavery movement were the Quakers. The Quakers were a religious group. They were the first to organize an antislavery society, way back in 1775, and they actively discouraged slaveholding by their members.

3. Slaves were free when they had reached the northernmost portion of their journey, where they would be supplied with food and a place to stay. But many did not feel safe even in the North because of the Fugitive Slave Law. This law said that slaves must be returned to their masters and that a person who helped slaves could also be jailed. So, some went on to Canada.

ANSWER KEY

1. B; 2. A; 3. C

B. Taking Notes: Using an Outline

○ Go over the directions.
○ Have students fill in the outline as you play the audio or video program. Repeat each section before continuing to the next.
○ Have students compare notes with a partner.

Audio Script

Section 1

Lecturer: Good morning. Nice to see you. O.K. Let's begin. Today I'm going to be giving you a little background on the Underground Railroad. [*indicates board*]

All right. The Underground Railroad was the name given to a movement in the United States during the 19th century. [*indicates board*] The 1800s. It was a movement that helped slaves gain their freedom. On the Underground Railroad, individuals escaped from slavery in the South to freedom in the North. There was no, uh, actual railroad or train on the Underground Railroad. Rather, it consisted of a series of, uh, houses that were called "stations." Slaves hid at these stations as they traveled from the South to the northern United States and, uh, sometimes even to Canada. More than 100,000 slaves escaped through the Underground Railroad.

The Underground Railroad began when individual slaves began to escape and find their way north. And, after a time, a number of northerners began to help the runaways, and the, uh, the movement became organized.

Now, where did the term *Underground Railroad* come from? It's not known when the term was first used, but it probably came into existence shortly after railroads became popular in the 1830s [*indicates board*]. However, slaves were escaping to the North long before then.

Section 2

Lecturer: Many people were involved in the Underground Railroad. It included a network of former slaves, um, free blacks, white Americans, and, uh, Canadians. Two organized groups that were involved in running the Underground Railroad were the abolitionists [*indicates board*] and the Quakers [*indicates board*].

A number of former slaves, such as Frederick Douglass, Harriet Tubman, and Sojourner Truth, supported the Undergound Railroad movement. Uh, you read about them in Chapter 23—right? That's Frederick Douglass, Harriet Tubman, and Sojourner Truth.

They were well known for speaking out against slavery, and, uh, Tubman became one of the most famous conductors of the railroad. By "conductor," I mean that she actually helped the slaves on their journey of escape from the South to the North. And there were also a number of free blacks who were abolitionists such as William Jones, Charles Lenox Remond, Henry Highland Garnet, William Wells Brown, and Francis E. W. Harper. They organized and raised funds to support the movement.

Now, the abolitionists were blacks and whites that were part of an organized movement against slavery. The most famous of the white abolitionists was William Lloyd Garrison, who established the first antislavery newspaper. Another abolitionist was Harriet Beecher Stowe. Stowe was the author of *Uncle Tom's Cabin.* In it, Stowe described the horrors of slavery. Many people in the North read it, and it made them aware of the evil of slavery. The Grimké sisters—that's G–R–I–M–K–E, with an accent on the "E"—uh, they were also well known abolitionists. They denounced their families' ownership of slaves and traveled around the country telling their story.

Another organized group in the antislavery movement were the Quakers. The Quakers were a religious group. They were the first to organize an antislavery society, way back in 1775, and they actively discouraged slaveholding by their members. They were also dedicated to helping ex-slaves by providing them with shelter, food, clothing, and money. Uh, Levi Coffin, a Quaker, he was known as "the president of the Underground Railroad" because of all the work he did in helping more than 3,000 slaves escape.

So, the Underground Railroad allowed white Americans a chance not only to speak out against the injustice of slavery but also to allow them to play an active role in *freeing* slaves.

Section 3

Lecturer: Now, what was a trip on the Underground Railroad like? Well, slaves would usually escape at night and travel along a route marked by others who had gone before them. Now, uh, normally, slaves would take supplies from their masters for the journey. The slaves traveled at night. They used the North Star as a guide, and on cloudy nights, the moss that grew on the northern part of the trees helped to guide them in the right direction.

The stations were only 10–20 miles apart because this was the maximum distance that most people walk at one time. During the day, the conductors—the uh, the people helping the slaves—would hide them in their barns or in secret places like cellars or attics until it was dark and safe for the slaves to leave. Slaves were free when they had reached the northernmost portion of their journey, where they would be supplied with food and a place to stay. But uh, many did not feel safe even in the North because of the Fugitive Slave Law [*indicates board*]. This law said that slaves must be returned to their masters and that a person who helped slaves could be jailed. So, some went on to Canada. There are some unusual escape stories. One of the most famous was that of Henry "Box" Brown. He traveled from Richmond, Virginia, to Philadelphia, Pennsylvania as freight in a box. It took him 26 hours to reach his destination, but at the end, he was free.

Section 4

Lecturer: Now, why was the Underground Railroad significant in the antislavery movement? There are two reasons. It's true that the Railroad was just one of the many strategies that abolitionists used to attack the system of slavery in the United States.

However, it was important because it proved that African Americans were not only committed to ending slavery, but also organized as a group to work against it. Of course, Harriet Tubman is the best example of the many African Americans who took action to win their own freedom. Her actions and that of other African Americans disproved the idea that slaves were unwilling to risk their lives for their own personal freedom or for the freedom of other slaves.

People who "traveled on the Underground Railroad" to freedom exposed the horrible system of slavery. Frederick Douglass's autobiography, along with the narratives of Venture Smith, William and Ellen Craft, and Henry "Box" Brown, are all good examples.

Their first-hand experiences worked a kind of antislavery publicity. Slaveholders viewed the Underground Railroad as a direct attack on the system of slavery. And the tremendous success of the Underground Railroad proved that the abolitionists were determined to destroy slavery.

O.K. I imagine there are plenty of questions. O.K., uh, yes, Mike?

ANSWER KEY

Section 1

I. The Underground Railroad
  A. It helped slaves <u>get their freedom</u>.
  B. Not a railroad, but a <u>series of houses that were called "stations."</u>
  C. The Underground Railroad began
    1. when: <u>1830s</u>
    2. how: <u>slaves began to escape, then northerners began to help the slaves and the movement became organized</u>

Section 2

II. Groups Involved in the Underground Railroad
  A. Individuals
    1. <u>Former slaves</u>
    2. Free blacks who were <u>abolitionists</u>
    3. White <u>abolitionists</u>
    4. <u>Quakers</u>
  B. Groups
    1. <u>Abolitionists</u>
    2. <u>Quakers</u>
  C. Reasons that whites were involved: gave them a chance to <u>speak out against the injustice of slavery and actually play a role in freeing slaves</u>

Section 3

III. A Trip on the Underground Railroad
  A. Supplies: <u>taken from master</u>
  B. Time of day: <u>at night</u>
  C. Guides: <u>the North Star, moss on trees</u>
  D. Stations: <u>10–20 miles apart</u>
  E. When slaves arrived in the North, they <u>were free</u>
  F. Henry "Box" Brown's story: <u>he traveled for 26 hours as freight in a box</u>

Section 4

IV. The Significance of the Underground Railroad
  A. It was a way to <u>attack</u> the system of slavery
  B. It proved that African Americans were willing to <u>organize as a group to work against slavery</u>

LISTENING STRATEGY: Listening for Examples in Groups

○ Go over the information in the box.
○ Ask questions: *What kind of examples are given in the categories in the lecture? What's a good way to take notes on categories and examples?*

TOEFL® iBT Tip

TOEFL iBT Tip 6: The TOEFL iBT listening comprehension section will require students to think critically about the conversations or lectures.

○ Point out that the listening strategy *Listening for Examples in Groups* will help students improve their critical thinking skills for the TOEFL iBT. Understanding how to organize notes and ideas into a chart will help students to connect and synthesize information in a lecture or conversation.

○ This skill can also be applied to tasks that require students to make a chart of information that they have heard.

C. Listening for Examples in Groups

○ Go over the directions.
○ Have students write the examples on the chart as you play the video or audio program.
○ Go over the answers with the class.

Audio Script

Lecturer: Many people were involved in the Underground Railroad. It included a network of former slaves, um, free blacks, white Americans, and, uh, Canadians. Two organized groups that were involved in running the Underground Railroad were the abolitionists [*indicates board*] and the Quakers [*indicates board*].

A number of former slaves, such as Frederick Douglass, Harriet Tubman, and Sojourner Truth, supported the Underground Railroad movement. Uh, you read about them in Chapter 23—right? That's Frederick Douglass, Harriet Tubman, and Sojourner Truth.

They were well known for speaking out against slavery, and, uh, Tubman became one of the most famous conductors of the railroad. By "conductor," I mean that she actually helped the slaves on their journey of escape from the South to the North. And there were also a number of free blacks who were abolitionists such as William Jones, Charles Lenox Remond, Henry Highland Garnet, William Wells Brown, and Francis E. W. Harper. They organized and raised funds to support the movement.

Now, the abolitionists were blacks and whites that were part of an organized movement against slavery. The most famous of the white abolitionists was William Lloyd Garrison, who established the first antislavery newspaper. Another abolitionist was Harriet Beecher Stowe. Stowe was the author of *Uncle Tom's Cabin.* In it, Stowe described the horrors of slavery. Many people in the North read it, and it made them aware of the evil of slavery. The Grimké sisters—that's G–R–I–M–K–E, with an accent on the "E"—uh, they were also well known abolitionists. They denounced their families' ownership of slaves and traveled around the country telling their story.

Another organized group in the antislavery movement were the Quakers. The Quakers were a religious group. They were the first to organize an antislavery society, way back in 1775, and they actively discouraged slaveholding by their members. They were also dedicated to helping ex-slaves by providing them with shelter, food, clothing, and money. Uh, Levi Coffin, a Quaker, he was known as "the president of the Underground Railroad" because of all the work he did in helping more than 3,000 slaves escape.

White Abolitionists	Quakers
William Lloyd Garrison Harriet Beecher Stowe Grimké sisters	Levi Coffin

LISTENING STRATEGY: Listening for Dates

○ Go over the information in the box.
○ Ask questions: *What is a good way to present information with dates? What should you listen for? What are some expressions that may introduce a date or time?*

🎧 D. Listening for Dates

○ Go over the directions.
○ Have students take notes on the timeline as you play the video or audio program.
○ Go over the answers with the class.

Audio Script

1. Another organized group in the antislavery movement were the Quakers. The Quakers were a religious group. They were the first to organize an antislavery society, way back in 1775, and they actively discouraged slaveholding by their members.
2. All right. The Underground Railroad was the name given to a movement in the United States during the nineteenth century.
3. Now, where did the term *Underground Railroad* come from? It's not known when the term was first used, but it probably came into existence shortly after railroads became popular in the 1830s. However, slaves were escaping to the North long before then.

ANSWER KEY

Ex-Slaves	Free Black Abolitionists
Frederick Douglass Harriet Tubman Sojourner Truth	William Jones Charles Lenox Remond Henry Highland Garnet William Wells Brown Francis E. W. Harper

ANSWER KEY

1775 – Quakers organized an anti-slavery society.
1800s – Underground Railroad movement
1830s – name *Underground Railroad* came into existence, railroads became popular

E. Checking Your Notes

- Go over the directions.
- Have students check their notes and fill in missing information as you play the audio or video program. Play all four sections without a break.
- Have students compare notes with a partner.
- Go over the answers with the class.

Audio Script

Use the script for Activity B on page 98 of the Teacher's Edition.

ANSWER KEY

Use the outline for Activity B on page 100 of the Teacher's Edition.

After Listening

A. Using Your Notes

- Go over the directions and the questions.
- Have students discuss the questions in pairs or small groups.
- Call on students to share their answers with the class.

ANSWER KEY

1. 1830s; 2. it came into existence soon after railroads became popular; 3. They wanted to help free slaves; 4. Slaves escaped and traveled at night, hiding in barns, cellars, or attics during the day; 5. They were free; 6. It showed that blacks were willing to organize against slavery

B. Making Connections

- Go over the directions and the questions. You may want to have students do the Expansion Activity that follows now.
- Have students discuss the question in small groups.
- Call on students to share their ideas with the class.

EXPANSION ACTIVITY: Comparing Chapter Sections

- Photocopy and distribute Worksheet BLM 8.
- Have students complete the Venn diagrams and compare diagrams with a partner.
- Call on students to share their ideas with the class.

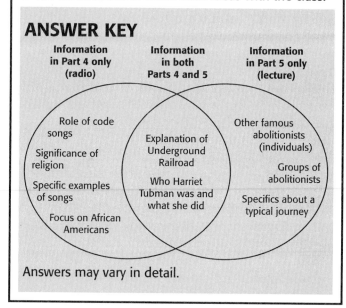

ANSWER KEY

| Information in Part 4 only (radio) | Information in both Parts 4 and 5 | Information in Part 5 only (lecture) |

- Role of code songs
- Significance of religion
- Specific examples of songs
- Focus on African Americans

- Explanation of Underground Railroad
- Who Harriet Tubman was and what she did

- Other famous abolitionists (individuals)
- Groups of abolitionists
- Specifics about a typical journey

Answers may vary in detail.

Put It All Together

- Go over the directions. Have students read through the steps.

SPEAKING STRATEGY: Working Cooperatively

- Go over the information in the box.
- Ask questions: *What is the best way to work in a group? What are some things a good group member should do? What is a job you might like to do in a group?*

Step 1

- Go over the directions and the example list of assignments.
- Put students in groups. Have each group brainstorm a list of topics and then choose one that most people in the group like.
- Elicit topics from the groups.

Steps 2 and 3

○ Go over the directions for Step 2 and the examples of key words and websites.
○ Go over the directions for Step 3.
○ Direct students' attention to the outline in Step 3.
○ Have students do research in the library and on the Internet. Remind students to complete their group assignments and to take notes on the outline.

Step 4

○ Go over the directions for Steps 4 and 5. Have students read the questions in Step 5. Point out that this may help groups in their presentations.
○ Have each group give a presentation to the class. Remind students to make eye contact.

SPEAKING STRATEGY: Giving and Getting Feedback

○ Go over the information in the box.
○ Ask questions: *What is feedback? Why is it a good idea to get feedback on a presentation? What kind of language and suggestions should you use to give feedback?*

EXPANSION ACTIVITY: Feedback Form

○ Photocopy and distribute the worksheet *Feedback Form* on page BLM 9. Cut along the lines to separate the forms, and give students enough copies to evaluate each group.
○ Have students complete the evaluations during the presentations.
○ Have groups collect and discuss the evaluations of their presentation.

Step 5

○ Go over the directions.
○ Ask each question and elicit feedback.

CRITICAL THINKING STRATEGY: Listening to Feedback

○ Responding appropriately to feedback is very important to success as a student. Using suggestions from teachers and classmates can greatly improve academic skills.
○ When receiving feedback, students may feel offended by suggestions to change their work. Try to look at criticism as an opportunity to improve, not as a personal insult.
○ Students can listen to feedback without following all of the speaker's advice. Even when students decide not to change their work after hearing feedback, it is still useful to hear what another person thinks about their work.
○ It is always polite to thank the person giving feedback, whether the feedback was positive or negative.

EXPANSION ACTIVITY: Reading Practice

○ Photocopy and distribute worksheet BLM 10.
○ Have students read the passage and do the activities.
○ Go over the answers with the class.

ANSWER KEY

1. 1820; 2. she thought she was going to be sold; 3. more than 300; 4. a head injury when she tried to help another slave; 5. she was a nurse, a spy, and a soldier

Events on timeline:
1820 – born in Maryland
1845 – married John Tubman
1849 – escaped
1860 – last journey on the Underground Railroad
1870 – married Nelson Davis
1913 – died

UNIT 3 ●●●●●● HISTORY

CHAPTER 6 U.S. HISTORY THROUGH FILM

In Part 1, students will read about three films (*Far and Away, The Missing,* and *Apollo 13*) by the American director Ron Howard. In Part 2, students will listen to a conversation about a film. In Part 4, students will listen to a radio program about Hollywood westerns (movies depicting the Old West in the United States). In Part 5, students will listen to a lecture on the origins of four film genres in different periods of U.S. history. Finally, students will create a project on images in film.

VOCABULARY

agrarian	despot	genre	plot	symbol
astronaut	evict	hardship	romanticize	synthesize
boundary	evil	heroine	roots	theme
box office	fading into the sunset	iconic	setting	universal
character	feel like	journey	shootout	western
characteristic	frontier	make a comeback	spaghetti western	wise
courage	generation	period	survey	

LISTENING STRATEGY
Review: Taking Lecture Notes

CRITICAL THINKING STRATEGIES
Interpreting Symbols (Part 1)
Synthesizing (Part 5)
Note: Strategy in bold is highlighted in the student book.

MECHANICS OF LISTENING AND SPEAKING
Pronunciation: Verbs Ending in –*ed*
Words In Phrases: Giving an Opinion
Language Function: Agreeing and Disagreeing
Intonation: Showing Disagreement with Intonation

SPEAKING STRATEGIES
Talking About Symbols
Taking a Survey

TEST-TAKING STRATEGY
Review: Taking Lecture Notes

CHAPTER 6 — U.S. History Through Film

Chapter 6 Opener, page 175

○ Direct students' attention to the photo and chapter title. Go over the directions and questions.
○ Put students in pairs to share their ideas.
○ Call on students to share their ideas with the class.

PART ① INTRODUCTION
RON HOWARD'S VISION OF U.S. HISTORY, PAGES 176–182

A. Thinking Aloud

○ Direct students' attention to the photos. Ask: *What movies do you see in the photos?*
○ Go over the directions and the questions.
○ Have students discuss the questions in pairs.
○ Call on students to share their ideas with the class.

ANSWER KEY

Answers will vary.

EXPANSION ACTIVITY: Category Sort

○ Tell students that you are going to ask some questions. They will respond by moving around the room to stand with classmates who have the same or similar answers. Point out that they should ask classmates the question in order to sort themselves by answer. Encourage students to form distinct groups according to the answers they give.
○ Ask a question: *What is your favorite type of movie?* Remind students to sort themselves by answer. When students have formed groups, call on someone from each group to tell the class their answer to the question (*Action, Comedy, etc.*).
○ Ask several more questions. Create your own or use these: *What is your favorite movie? What was the last movie you saw? Who is your favorite director? Who is your favorite actor?*

B. Reading

○ Direct students' attention to the article on page 177.
○ Go over the directions and the questions.
○ Have students read the article and think about the question.
○ Elicit answers to the questions.

ANSWER KEY

Far and Away depicts immigration from Ireland to America, *The Missing* depicts the opening of the American frontier, and *Apollo 13* depicts a 1970 trip to the moon. The three films reflect the values of honesty, courage, family, hard work, and perseverance.

Culture Note

○ Before he became a director, Ron Howard was a well-known child actor. His television roles as Opie on *The Andy Griffith Show* and the teenager Richie on *Happy Days* represented the life of the typical "All-American" boy. For this reason, his movies remind many Americans of the traditional life of their childhood.

Academic Note

○ Point out the importance of format in a reading, especially the use of italics and words in bold. Explain or elicit that the italics in this passage are used to indicate a title (e.g., *Far and Away*), foreign words (e.g., *anime*), and for emphasis (e.g., *heroine*). Words in bold indicate a passage heading or a special vocabulary word.

C. Vocabulary Check

○ Go over the directions.
○ Have students write the words or phrases on the lines and then compare answers with a partner.
○ Go over the answers with the class.

ANSWER KEY

1. genre; 2. universal; 3. evicts; 4. journey; 5. hardships;
6. evil; 7. symbol; 8. boundaries; 9. western; 10. frontier;
11. astronauts; 12. courage

D. Comparing and Contrasting

○ Go over the directions and the words and phrases in the box.
○ Have students write the words and phrases in the chart and then compare answers with a partner.
○ Go over the answers with the class.

ANSWER KEY

Far and Away	The Missing	Apollo 13	All three films
disappearing social classes the dream of owning land immigrants to the U.S.	a female hero finding a family member	danger on a trip to the moon	family courage hard work honesty perseverance journey

TOEFL® iBT Tip

TOEFL iBT Tip 1: The TOEFL iBT listening comprehension section will challenge students to think critically about the conversations or lectures that they hear and to organize their notes in a way that will help them synthesize information.

○ Point out that the activity *Comparing and Contrasting* will help students understand how to organize notes and ideas into a chart. This will help them to connect information from a lecture or conversation to the information in a reading text and respond to it in spoken or written form.

E. Discussion

○ Go over the directions.
○ Have students discuss the questions in small groups.
○ Call on students to share their ideas with the class.

ANSWER KEY

Answers will vary.

SPEAKING STRATEGY: Talking about Symbols

○ Go over the information in the box.
○ Ask questions: *What is a symbol? What are some expressions we can use to talk about symbols?*

F. Talking about Symbols

○ Go over the directions and the example.
○ Have students think of their own symbol to write in the bottom row of the chart.
○ Have students talk to three classmates about the symbols and write the answers in the chart.
○ Call on students to tell the class about their classmates' opinions about one symbol.

ANSWER KEY

Answers will vary.

Culture Notes

○ In the U.S., a star might represent something excellent or famous, like a movie star.
○ A tree often represents a family or nature.
○ A road might represent going on a journey, or the "journey" of a person's life.
○ Blue usually represents sadness in the U.S.
○ Red usually represents anger, but also has many other meanings, including romance and embarrassment.
○ A dove almost always represents peace in the U.S.
○ In the U.S., a white flag represents surrender.

CRITICAL THINKING STRATEGY: Interpreting Symbols

○ To understand symbols, it is important to know the culture of the speaker. Symbols can have opposite meanings for different cultures.
○ Listen to the speaker's intonation to learn how the speaker feels about the image.

EXPANSION ACTIVITY: Personal Symbols

○ Ask students to choose a symbol that they think symbolizes who they are.
○ Have students draw their symbol and then explain it to a partner.
○ Call on students to tell the class about their partner's symbol.

G. Journal Writing

○ Go over the directions.
○ Explain that this is a freewriting activity and does not have to be perfect. Point out that journal writing can be a warm-up to a more structured writing assignment, helping to generate ideas.
○ Set a time limit of five minutes.
○ Put students in pairs to read or talk about their writing.

PART ② SOCIAL LANGUAGE
HOLLYWOOD AND STEREOTYPES, PAGES 182–185

Before Listening
A. Thinking Ahead

○ Direct students' attention to the photos on page 182. Ask questions: *What kind of movies are these? What do the movies say about the place and time in the photos?*
○ Go over the directions and the questions.
○ Have students discuss the questions in small groups.
○ Call on students to share their ideas with the class.

ANSWER KEY

1. Answers will vary; 2. The cowboys were usually the heroes and the Indians were usually the "bad guys."
3. In recent westerns, white people learn to understand the Native American culture.

B. Guessing the Meaning from Context

○ Go over the directions.
○ Have students write the meaning of the words in red.
○ Go over the answers with the class.

ANSWER KEY

1. be in the mood for; 2. intelligent

Listening
 A. Listening for the Main Idea

○ Go over the directions and the questions.
○ Play the video or audio program.
○ Ask students: *Do Tanya and Jennifer agree about Dances with Wolves? Why?*

Audio Script

Jennifer: That's a sad movie.
Tanya: Uh-huh.
Jennifer: This is the third time I've seen it, and I cry every time.
Tanya: You want some ice cream?
Jennifer: Ice cream? How can you think about ice cream now, after *Dances with Wolves*?
Tanya: Well, I'm hungry, and I feel like some mint chocolate chip.
Jennifer: You didn't think that movie was depressing?
Tanya: Not really. I mean, I know it was supposed to be sad, but I just didn't think it was very good.
Jennifer: But think about all those cowboy and Indian movies from the past. The cowboys were always the good guys, the Indians were always the bad guys, and—
Tanya: True, but—
Jennifer: Isn't it nice to finally see the Indians as the good guys?
Tanya: I'm not sure. I mean, I know those old movies were pretty terrible. But this really isn't any better. It just takes away one stereotype and puts a new stereotype in its place.
Jennifer: What do you mean?
Tanya: Well, think about it. What's a stereotype, anyway? An idea about a group of people that's too simple, right? An idea that isn't realistic, right?
Jennifer: Yeah, but—
Tanya: So in the old movies, all the Indians were evil, lazy, violent, dirty, dangerous, stupid. And now, huh, they're all good, gentle, loving, and wise. Pretty picture, but it isn't realistic. Nobody is all bad or all good.
Jennifer: OK, I guess you have a point. But I think it's good for people to learn how horrible we were to the Indians in the last century—how we took the land, we killed the buffalo, we brought disease—

Tanya: Whoa, girl! What's this *we*? It wasn't *my* people that did that stuff. It was *your* people.

Jennifer: Yeah. O.K. Anyway, people need to know how bad it was for the Indians.

Tanya: Until the big white movie star came and saved them, right?

Jennifer: I feel like some chocolate chip mint. How about you?

ANSWER KEY

Tanya and Jennifer don't agree; Jennifer liked the movie and Tanya didn't. Tanya thought it just replaced one stereotype with another.

TOEFL® iBT Tip

TOEFL iBT Tip 2: The TOEFL iBT measures the ability to understand the main idea or purpose and important details of a conversation or a lecture.

○ Point out that the activity *Listening for the Main Idea* helps students improve their overall basic comprehension skills.

○ On the TOEFL iBT, main idea questions may appear in the following formats:
   What are the speakers mainly discussing?
   Why does the student want to talk to the professor?

 B. Listening for Stressed Words

○ Go over the directions.
○ Have students put accent marks over stressed words as you play the video or audio program.
○ Put students in pairs to compare answers.
○ Go over the answers with the class.
○ Explain to students that perception of stress may vary from person to person.

Audio Script

Jennifer: That's a *sad* movie!

Tanya: Uh-huh.

Jennifer: This is the *third* time I've seen it, and I *cry* every time.

Tanya: You want some *ice cream*?

Jennifer: Ice cream? How can you think about ice cream *now*, after *Dances with Wolves*?

Tanya: Well, I'm *hungry*, and I feel like some mint chocolate chip.

Jennifer: You didn't think that movie was *depressing*?

Tanya: Not really. I mean, I know it was supposed to be sad, but I just didn't think it was very *good*.

Jennifer: But *think* about all those cowboy and Indian movies from the past. The cowboys were always the good guys; the Indians were always the bad guys.

Tanya: True, but—

Jennifer: Isn't it nice to finally see the *Indians* as the *good* guys?

Tanya: I'm not sure. I mean, I *know* those old movies were pretty *terrible.* But this really isn't any better. It just takes away one stereotype and puts a *new* stereotype in its place.

ANSWER KEY

Answers will vary. Possible answers include:
sad; third; cry; ice cream; hungry; depressing; good; think; good; Indians; know; terrible; new

 C. Listening for a Definition

○ Go over the directions.
○ Have students write the definition as you play the video or audio program.
○ Go over the answers with the class.

Audio Script

Tanya: Well, think about it. What's a stereotype anyway? An idea about a group of people that's too simple, right? An idea that isn't realistic, right?

ANSWER KEY

An idea about a group of people that's too simple and isn't realistic.

 D. Listening for Examples of Stereotypes

○ Go over the directions.
○ Have students write the examples of stereotypes in the chart as you play the video or audio program.
○ Have students compare their charts with a partner.
○ Go over the answers with the class.

Audio Script

Tanya: So in the old movies, all the Indians were evil, lazy, violent, dirty, dangerous and stupid. And now, huh, they're all good, gentle, loving, and wise. Pretty picture, but it isn't realistic. Nobody is all bad or all good.

ANSWER KEY

From Old Movies	From New Movies
evil	good
lazy	gentle
violent	loving
dirty	wise
dangerous	
stupid	

 E. Listening for Reasons

○ Go over the directions.
○ Have students write their answers as you play the video or audio program again.
○ Have students compare answers with a partner.
○ Go over the answers with the class.

Audio Script

Use the script for Activity A on page 107 of the Teacher's Edition.

ANSWER KEY

Jennifer thinks it's good because it shows the Indians as the good guys, and it's good for people to learn how horrible the white people were to the Indians, taking the land, killing the buffalo, and bringing disease. Tanya thinks it's bad because it just takes away one stereotype and puts a new stereotype in its place.

After Listening

A. Gathering Ideas

○ Go over the directions.
○ Have students make notes on their answers to the questions.

B. Discussing Stereotypes

○ Go over the directions.
○ Have students discuss the questions in small groups.
○ Call on representatives from each group to report on one of the stereotypes they discussed.

PART ③ THE MECHANICS OF LISTENING AND SPEAKING, PAGES 185–188

PRONUNCIATION: Verbs Ending in –ed

○ Go over the information in the box. Play the audio program.
○ Ask comprehension questions: *What are three ways that –ed can be pronounced? What is an example of a voiceless consonant? A voiced consonant?*

Pronunciation Note

○ You may want to point out that students can distinguish between voiced and voiceless consonants if they put their hands on their throats as they make the consonant sound. Voiced consonants will make the throat vibrate, but voiceless consonants do not.

A. Hearing Verbs Ending in *-ed*
- Go over the directions and the example.
- Have students check the correct pronunciation as you play the audio program.
- Go over the answers with the class.

Audio Script
1. turned	7. joked	13. loved
2. dropped	8. agreed	14. watched
3. laughed	9. killed	15. pointed
4. poured	10. saved	16. looked
5. needed	11. passed	17. studied
6. explained	12. repeated	18. appreciated

ANSWER KEY
1. /d/ 2. /t/ 3. /t/ 4. /d/ 5. /Id/ 6. /d/ 7. /t/ 8. /d/ 9. /d/ 10. /d/ 11. /t/ 12. /Id/ 13. /d/ 14. /t/ 15. /Id/ 16. /Id/ 17. /d/ 18. /Id/

B. Repeating Verbs Ending in *-ed*
- Go over the directions.
- Have students repeat the words as you play the audio program.

Audio Script
worked	worried	treated
crossed	answered	treated
washed	handled	sounded
fixed	climbed	listed

C. Pronouncing Verbs Ending in *-ed*
- Go over the directions.
- Have students work in pairs to say the words and write the pronunciation on the lines.
- Have students correct their answers as you play the audio program.

Audio Script
1. hoped	8. wanted	15. packed
2. accepted	9. covered	16. pushed
3. liked	10. painted	17. nodded
4. happened	11. traded	18. thanked
5. included	12. carried	19. represented
6. played	13. traveled	20. toured
7. called	14. added	21. listened

ANSWER KEY
1. /t/; 2. /Id/; 3. /t/; 4. /d/; 5. /Id/; 6. /d/; 7. /d/; 8. /Id/; 9. /d/; 10. /Id/; 11. /Id/; 12. /d/; 13. /d/; 14. /Id/; 15. /t/; 16. /t/; 17. /Id/; 18. /t/; 19. /Id/; 20. /d/; 21. /d/

WORDS IN PHRASES: Giving an Opinion
- Go over the information in the box.
- Ask comprehension questions: *What expressions can we use to introduce an opinion? What follows the expressions?*

TOEFL® iBT Tip

TOEFL iBT Tip 3: The independent speaking task on the TOEFL iBT may require examinees to state and defend an opinion on a particular subject.

- Point out that the activity *Giving an Opinion* will help students to learn phrases such as *I think, it seems to me that, in my opinion, if you ask me . . .* to give an opinion clearly and succinctly.

- Mention that these phrases are also useful for identifying a speaker's opinions in the listening comprehension section of the test.

D. Words in Phrases
- Go over the directions.
- Have students work in pairs to practice giving opinions about the topics. Remind students to use the expressions in the box.
- Call on students to share their ideas about one of the topics with the class.

LANGUAGE FUNCTIONS: Agreeing and Disagreeing

○ Go over the information in the box.
○ Ask questions: *What is one way to express agreement? What is one way to express disagreement politely?*

E. Agreeing and Disagreeing

○ Go over the directions.
○ Put students in pairs to take turns giving opinions on the topics and agreeing or disagreeing.

EXPANSION ACTIVITY: Vote with Your Feet

○ Write *Agree* on one side of the board and *Disagree* on the other.
○ Explain the activity. You will say a sentence and students should stand near the word that expresses their opinion.
○ Call a group of students to the board. Say *English is a very difficult language to learn.* Remind students to stand near *Agree* or *Disagree.*
○ Ask students to explain their position.
○ Say other sentences. Use your own or the ones below. You may want to have different groups of students come to the board.
 Americans aren't interested in learning other languages.
 The best movies don't use stereotypes.
 Stereotypes do not accurately represent a group of people.
 A good story is more important than believable characters in a movie.

🎧 INTONATION: Showing Disagreement with Intonation

○ Go over the information in the box. Play the audio program.
○ Ask: *How is the intonation different when someone actually disagrees?* (Many answers are possible.)

🎧 F. Understanding Intonation

○ Go over the directions.
○ Have students circle the correct answer as you play the audio program.
○ Have students compare answers with a partner.
○ Go over the answers with the class.

Audio Script

1. **A:** He's a wonderful actor.
 B: True! [*Agree*]
2. **A:** That movie is completely unrealistic.
 B: I see your point . . . [*Disagree*]
3. **A:** The American government broke almost every promise to the Indians.
 B: Well, that's true. [*Agree*]
4. **A:** We should visit a reservation over summer vacation.
 B: Yeah! [*Agree*]
5. **A:** It's just another stereotype.
 B: That's a good point . . . [*Disagree*]
6. **A:** You know, the whites weren't the only ones who killed buffalo. The Plains Indians killed them all the time.
 B: Well, that's true . . . [*Disagree*]
7. **A:** You know, the government almost always moved Native Americans to reservations on really terrible land.
 B: That's a good point. [*Agree*]
8. **A:** Native American jewelry is beautiful, but it's very expensive.
 B: True . . . [*Disagree*]

ANSWER KEY

1. agree; 2. disagree; 3. agree; 4. agree; 5. disagree; 6. disagree; 7. agree; 8. disagree

---

🎧 G. Using Intonation

○ Go over the directions.
○ Have students repeat the second person's response as you play the audio program again.

Audio Script

Use the script for Activity F above.

Put It Together
Giving and Responding to Opinions
❍ Go over the directions and the examples.
❍ Direct students' attention to the topics.
❍ Model the activity. Call on a student to play the role of Student B. Give an opinion on one of the topics (e.g., *I think* The Lord of the Rings *was a great movie. I watched it three times.*). Elicit agreement or disagreement from the student.
❍ Put students in pairs to talk about the topics. Remind students to pronounce past tense endings correctly and to express agreement or disagreement only with intonation.
❍ Walk around to monitor the activity and provide help as needed.

EXPANSION ACTIVITY: Movie Review Letters
❍ Have students choose a movie.
❍ Tell students to write a letter to a friend in which they summarize a movie, either recommend that the friend see it or not, and give reasons.
❍ Collect the letters and redistribute.
❍ Call on students to read a letter to the class. Elicit agreement or disagreement with the opinions expressed in the letters.

PART  BROADCAST ENGLISH
HOLLYWOOD WESTERNS MAKE A COMEBACK, PAGES 189–191

Before Listening
A. Thinking Ahead
❍ Go over the directions and the questions.
❍ Have students discuss the questions in small groups.
❍ Call on students to share their ideas with the class.

ANSWER KEY
Answers will vary.
1. They are all brave, action-oriented, and independent. They all use some kind of violence to fight bad guys.
2. kids and young adult men
3. Italy, because spaghetti comes from Italy.
4. more action movies were set in the future, in space
5. Answer will vary.
6. Answer will vary.
7. Answer will vary.

Culture Notes
❍ A *gunslinger* is a common character in western movies—movies about life in the western part of America in the 19th century C.E. A gunslinger is a solitary hero who fights with a gun. He usually rides a horse.
❍ *Cop* is a slang term for a policeman.
❍ A *knight* is a warrior from medieval European history (roughly the 5th to the 15th centuries C.E.). Real knights were landowners who fought on horseback, but knights in legends are heroes who wear shining armor and fight magical monsters like dragons.
❍ In the 1950s and 1960s, many westerns were made in Italy. They were called "spaghetti westerns" because spaghetti comes from Italy.

B. Vocabulary Preparation
❍ Go over the directions.
❍ Have students write the correct words or phrases on the lines.
❍ Go over the answers with the class.

ANSWER KEY
1. romanticize; 2. fading into the sunset; 3. generation; 4. shootout; 5. box office; 6. despot

EXPANSION ACTIVITY: Beanbag Toss

○ Tell students they have one minute to review the vocabulary.

○ After one minute, ask students to close their books.

○ Tell students that you will call on a student and toss a beanbag or ball. You will say one of the definitions, and the students should respond with the vocabulary word or phrase and throw the beanbag back.

○ Call on a student and toss the beanbag, saying *a fight with guns.* Elicit an answer from the student (*a shootout*) and have them toss the beanbag or ball back to you.

○ Repeat with other students. This is a fast-paced activity.

Listening

Culture Notes

○ Walter Hill was born in 1942. He worked in oil drilling and construction before he became an assistant director in 1967. He has written, directed, and produced over 20 films, many of which were westerns or had western themes.

○ Dialogue from the movie *Shane* is included in the interview. *Shane,* filmed in 1953, is the story of a gunslinger who wants to stop fighting. He tries to live with a peaceful family, but gets involved in a conflict between ranchers and farmers. He becomes a fighter again and says goodbye to the family he loves.

○ In the scene from *Shane,* the word *brand* is used to mean a mark made on skin with a hot metal instrument. Cowboys used brands to mark the cattle that belonged to them, but in the distant past, brands were also used to mark the faces of criminals so that everyone would know that they were guilty.

🎧 A. Listening for the Main Idea: Section 1

○ Go over the directions.

○ Have students write the answer to the question as you play the audio program.

Audio Script

Inskeep: The Hollywood western is making a comeback, or riding back into town, or getting back on the train or however you want to put it. The movie *Open Range* is out. Director Ron Howard has a western coming out this fall. John Woo plans to makes a western about Chinese workers building the Transcontinental Railroad. Pat Dowell reports on the latest episode for an art form that dates back to the last days of the Old West itself.

Dowell: Audiences for westerns have always been male, but they also used to be what is now Hollywood's target audience, teenage males who'll see a movie more than once. From 1903 when *The Great Train Robbery* was released up to World War II, audiences loved westerns so much that one out of every five movies made in the United States was a western. Director Walter Hill says the biggest reason that westerns started fading into the sunset in the 1960s was because the stories and the settings they romanticized began disappearing from living memory.

Hill: The broad audience was no longer identifying with their agrarian roots of American history, American past. And I think the generation before that, whether by direct experience or through their parents or grandparents, they had a great identity with what we used to call the making of the West and that being in touch with that history. And they weren't nearly as urban.

Dowell: Hill directed the western *The Long Riders* in 1980 and in the 1990s, *Geronimo* and *Wild Bill,* both of which failed at the box office. He's made other kinds of movies too, such as *48 Hours,* but he once famously said that all his movies are westerns.

ANSWER KEY

The stories and settings (places) in Westerns began disappearing from human memory. The audience no longer identified with their agrarian roots (that is, they no longer felt closely connected to their families' history as farmers).

B. Listening for the Main Idea: Section 2
○ Go over the directions.
○ Have students answer the question as you play the audio program.

Audio Script

Dowell: *The Wild Bunch,* one of the greatest westerns of all time, is about to be remade as an urban crime thriller. Walon Green earned an Oscar nomination for co-writing the original 1969 movie. Green won an Emmy writing for *NYPD Blue* and now produces the new TV *Dragnet.* Both cowboys and cops seem to him to share something with the knights errant of old.

Green: They come, they do some amazing service; they either kill a dragon, they kill the bad guy, whatever they do, and they move on. The traditional western hero—and probably my favorite western actually is *Shane,* and it's a great example of that—is that the western hero comes—he lives actually in this family but you know no matter how much they like him, he will not ever be part of the family.

[Audio from Shane]

Brandon De Wilde [*As Joey Starrett*]: We want you, Shane.

Alan Ladd [*As Shane*]: Joey, there's no living with, with the killing. There's no going back. Right or wrong, it's a brand. A brand sticks. There's no going back. Now you run on home to your mother and tell her—tell her everything's all right and there aren't any more guns in the valley.

Dowell: Like the gunslinger, cops are outsiders who come in to clean up the town but not socialize, says Green.

Green: They're the people that—we bring them in when we need things done that either we can't do or they're too unpleasant to do. And we basically pay them or hire them or coerce them or whatever to do it. And they do it. And then when they've done it we don't particularly want to know them and they don't particularly want to know us.

Dowell: *Open Range* is a very traditional American western in the line of John Ford, says historian Scott Simmon. It harks back to the days before Clint Eastwood went to Europe to become a star in spaghetti westerns.

Simmon: Although *Open Range* tells a kind of traditional story, it's one that feels to me a little more dangerous to tell now which is that if you have a despot who is causing trouble, that if you get out your guns and have a shootout, the problems are solved and there's nothing really to be said afterwards.

You know, that's the story the western always tells and it's not particularly unique. But, you know, it's a question of whether it needs to be told again right now.

Dowell: The questions *Open Range* raises are still the old ones usually asked by the women in the movie: How long before they ride out of the valley and will all the guns go with them? For NPR News this is Pat Dowell.

Inskeep: It's 11 minutes before the hour.

ANSWER KEY

They come, they do an amazing service (kill a dragon, kill the bad guy) and move on.

C. Listening for Details: Section 1
○ Go over the directions.
○ Have students write the answers as you play the audio program.

Audio Script

Use the script for Activity A on page 113 of the Teacher's Edition.

ANSWER KEY

1. teenage males; 2. one out of every five; 3. all his movies are westerns

D. Listening for Details: Section 2
○ Go over the directions.
○ Have students write the answers as you play the audio program.

Audio Script
○ Use the script for Activity B above.

ANSWER KEY

1. They are outsiders who come in to clean up the town but not socialize.
2. A despot is causing trouble, and if you get out your guns and have a shootout, the problems are solved.

TOEFL® iBT Tip

TOEFL iBT Tip 4: The TOEFL iBT measures the ability to understand the main idea and important details of a conversation or lecture.

○ Point out that the *Listening for Details* activity helps students to improve their overall basic comprehension skills for the TOEFL iBT. Students will need to review and practice these types of questions many times in preparation for the test.

After Listening

A. Comprehension Check

○ Have students compare their answers to Listening Activities A–D with a partner.
○ Go over the answers with the class.

B. Discussion

○ Go over the directions and the questions.
○ Put students in small groups to discuss the questions.
○ Call on students to share their ideas with the class.

ANSWER KEY

Answers will vary.

EXPANSION ACTIVITY: Apply Your Knowledge

○ Review the elements of the western (someone comes in to fight, to clean up a situation, doesn't get too close to the other people).
○ Put students in small groups to list three non-westerns that share these elements.
○ Call on students to share their ideas with the class.

PART ⑤ ACADEMIC ENGLISH
U.S. History Through
Film, pages 192–198

Before Listening
A. Thinking Ahead

○ Go over the directions.
○ Direct students' attention to the photos and ask: *What do you see? What kind of movies are these?*
○ Have students discuss the questions in small groups.
○ Call on students to share their ideas with the class.

ANSWER KEY

Answers will vary. *Monument Valley* is a western, *Top Hat* is a musical, and *Rain Man* is a drama.

TEST-TAKING STRATEGY: Review: Taking Lecture Notes

○ Go over the information in the box.
○ Ask: *What are some things you can do to take good notes? What forms can you use? What expressions introduce important ideas?*

TOEFL® iBT Tip

TOEFL iBT Tip 5: Because the TOEFL iBT now allows note-taking, students need to learn the best strategies to take notes quickly and effectively.

○ Remind students that the test-taking strategy *Taking Lecture Notes* can help them to identify important information. The ability to organize notes efficiently can help learners make connections between the major and minor points in a lecture or conversation.

○ Encourage students to think about their personal note-taking styles: Do they like to draw charts? Do they prefer to construct outlines? It is best to be familiar with many note-taking styles, but focus on the one that is most comfortable.

Listening

🎙️🎧 A. Taking Lecture Notes: Using an Outline

❍ Go over the directions.
❍ Have students fill in the outline as you play the video or audio program.
❍ Have students compare answers with a partner.
❍ Go over the answers with the class.

Audio Script

Lecturer: O.K. Hi guys. Guys? Um, we need to get started here. O.K. Thanks.

As you know, this week we're on U.S. history as seen through film. Everyone likes movies, right? Well, one great thing about movies is that they can help you remember things you learn in class. You study some historical period or event in class, and a picture comes into your mind—an image from some movie you saw once maybe when you were a kid. These images—these vivid pictures that stay in your mind from movies—these are called "iconic images." I'll say that term again 'cause you're gonna hear it a lot in this lecture. Iconic images. I–C–O–N–I–C. Got that? Good. Iconic images are a kind of symbol. They represent a bigger idea.

O.K., let me review from last time. Does everyone remember the word *genre*? Right. A genre is a type or *form* of film. Every film in the same genre shares certain similar, familiar characteristics. Did I go through this list last time? No? O.K., well, lemme give you a quick list of these characteristics. Films in the same genre have *one or more* of these. First, setting—in other words, where the movie takes place. Next, subject or theme—what it's about. Third, period. *When* does it take place? Fourth, plot or story. Next, certain familiar characters—you know, like the good guy, the bad guy, the beautiful young girl, and so on. And last, there are shared iconic images—these pictures that stay in the mind of the audience. So how many of these characteristics did I list? Six? O.K. Well, there are more, but let's leave it at that.

Um, before we get into the two historical periods for today, let me review from last time. I was talking about historical dramas, and one type of historical drama is the immigration story. You have something like *Far and Away,* which takes place around 1845 and shows the hardships of Irish immigrants. But these immigration stories aren't always dramas, and they don't always

take place a long time ago. What's that movie with Tom Hanks—you know, the one in the airport from maybe 2004 or so? Yeah—*The Terminal.* Here we have not a drama but a romantic comedy about this guy from some Eastern European country who's stuck in a New York airport for *months.* The point is that immigration is a natural subject for American films because it has always been an important part of U.S. history.

Section 2

Lecturer: Last time, I spoke a little about the period that we call "The Wild West." I need to continue with that today because the iconic images are so much a part of American culture. Lemme give a quick definition. When we say "The Wild West," we're referring not only to a place but also to a time. The place was the huge area west of the Mississippi River, although in movies it's usually a more specific region: the areas that today are Texas, New Mexico, Colorado, Wyoming, places like that. The time was very short—from only about 1865, which was the end of the Civil War between the North and the South, to about 1900 or maybe 1910. Not long. A short period. But the images from that time are central to the American national identity.

O.K., that's where and when. Now, *what?* What was happening during this period? Well, after the Civil War, two railroad companies built train tracks across the country. It was hard, dangerous work. One company built from east to west. Many of the workers were immigrants—most of them Irish. The other company built from west to east. Many of those workers were also immigrants—most of them Chinese. Finally, in 1869, they joined up and finished the track, and people could cross from one end of the country to the other in, oh, a week or so instead of *months.*

Because of the railroad, more and more people began to move to the west. They came for a lot of reasons. Any ideas on this? Well, many came for land. Back in Europe, where most of them came from, they were farmers but couldn't own their own land. Here, that dream seemed possible. And they came for other reasons—gold, silver, even *adventure.* The point is that there was this idea that life might be better over *there,* someplace further west, someplace new.

Because so many people were moving west, small towns began to appear everywhere—especially where people discovered gold or silver. Suddenly there was this really busy little town, for example, full of thousands of people, and then, when the gold or silver ran out, the people moved on to a different place, and the town disappeared. But with all these people moving around, most of them strangers to one another, the problem was lack of *law.* Most of these towns didn't have any police. So that's why we call it the "wild" west. It was exciting and full of opportunity, but it was also pretty dangerous.

O.K. So movies about this period are called westerns, right? Westerns, like any other genre, share certain elements. First, most westerns are simple morality stories—in other words, they're about the conflict between good and evil. Second, there's always a hero and a villain, or bad guy—sometimes *guys,* and there's almost always a heroine—a beautiful young woman. Third, all westerns are action stories. They have violence and chase scenes on horses. And fourth, the theme of most westerns is pretty much the same. It's either about the dangers of moving west or about the hero who saves a town from the villains, the bad guys.

Now, remember those iconic images? Well, I want you to bring to your mind any western that you've ever seen. Just imagine it in your head. What do you see? Are you picturing it? *Those* are the iconic images. You have the image of the cowboy, of course. He's alone. He's riding a horse. The only things he owns are his clothing and a gun. He's wearing boots and jeans and a cowboy hat. And he's always on the move, right? Never stays in one place. Part of this image is the symbol of the cowboy hat. If the guy is wearing a white hat, what do you know about him? Right. He's our hero. He's the good guy. And a black hat? He's the bad guy. Of course, you know that this image is a complete stereotype, right? But that's not something we need to consider right now.

O.K. Two more iconic images. There's the shootout. And what's that? On the main street of the little town, you see two men, two cowboys, one in a black hat, one in a white hat. They stand facing each other, oh, about forty feet apart. They're tense. They're each wearing two guns—one on each hip. In just a minute, they're going to pull out their guns and shoot at each other. Only one will survive. Have you all seen this? Great. Now, I think you can figure out the symbolic meaning of this image, so I don't need to tell you.

One more iconic image from westerns: the land itself. It's huge. It's vast. It goes on forever and ever. Even our hero, the cowboy, is seen as very small against this enormous background. And this image is important. Why? It's symbolic of endless possibilities.

Section 3

Lecturer: Today I'm going to jump ahead to cover one more historical period that actually led to *several* film genres. That period is the Great Depression, from the year 1929 to about 1940. Lemme start with a quick history of the time. Well, just before this time, the 1920s were a time of great prosperity. People had money. Life was good. Then came 1929. The stock market crashed, and suddenly everyone lost their money. Well, almost everyone. Anyway, the 1930s were years when many, many people were very poor and hungry. The Depression was also the time of Prohibition. Prohibition was a law from Congress that made alcohol illegal, so people couldn't drink whiskey, wine, beer, anything alcoholic. But many people still *did* drink because there was a huge amount of organized crime. The criminals, called gangsters, secretly brought alcohol in from other countries or made it themselves. Clearly, Prohibition was not a success, and in 1933, Congress changed its mind and made alcohol legal again.

I need to mention one significant government action during the Depression. The U.S. government wanted to help the poor people and improve the economy, so they started a program called the W.P.A. This stands for the Works Progress Administration. It gave jobs to thousands of homeless, jobless people. Two good things happened. One: people had jobs. Two: they improved the country. For example, they built post offices and built bridges. They also built roads all across the country.

O.K. How do movies reflect this time? There are three important film genres that come from this period, and these genres still exist in many movies today.

First, there were musicals. Musicals were an important form of escape for a country in the middle of an economic depression. These were big, expensive, happy Hollywood productions with singing and dancing and amazing costumes. A typical plot, or story, in these musicals involves a poor young woman who has a little job as a singer or dancer in some production. The star of the production, who is not a nice person, gets sick or has some accident, and the young woman takes her place. She becomes an immediate success—and rich and famous. Examples of such films are *42nd Street* (from 1933) and *Top Hat* (from 1935). Perhaps the most famous iconic image of this genre is the elegant dancing couple of Fred Astaire and Ginger Rogers.

Long after the Depression ended, musicals remained as an important part of American culture. Think of such films as *Singing in the Rain* (from 1952), *A Chorus Line* (1985), or *Chicago* (2002).

The second genre is the crime drama. As you can imagine, all those gangsters during Prohibition were common characters in movies. One of the iconic images of this genre is the gangster wearing an expensive suit with a hat pulled over one eye and holding a gun. One of the famous crime dramas from this time was *Public Enemy,* from 1931. This type of movie has been popular ever since then. Think of *Bonnie and Clyde,* from 1967 or *The Godfather,* from 1972.

The third genre is an especially American form: the road trip. Remember those WPA projects I mentioned, when people got jobs building roads all over the country? Well, all those roads made it possible to move around the country easily, by car, and Hollywood began to make movies about people on grand journeys—sometimes funny, sometimes tragic. All of these films, like musicals, provided something that people needed in the Depression: escape from their problems. The first famous road trip movie was *It Happened One Night,* a wonderful, funny story about a rich young woman who runs away from home and the jobless newspaper writer who joins her. Like many Depression movies, the idea is that love wins over class differences. At the end of the Depression came the famous 1940 film *The Grapes of Wrath,* which told the story of poor homeless farmers moving from Oklahoma to California to try to find work. Road trip films, like musicals and crime dramas, are still popular today. Think of *Rain Man,* from 1988, or *Thelma and Louise,* from 1991. The point is that they all share the iconic image of people in a car on an endless road through the desert—and this sounds very similar to what? Right. That image of the *land* from westerns—land that goes on forever and ever.

And this brings me to my last point. Many, many movies fall into more than one genre. They're both westerns and road trips. They're both road trips and crime dramas. O.K. So for homework, after you read Chapter 7, I want you to think of five movies that fall into more than one genre. See you next week, when we're on to *Italian* history through film. Have a good weekend.

ANSWER KEY

Section 1

1.
New Term		Definition
Iconic image	=	vivid pictures that stay in your mind

2. **Characteristics of films in the same genre:**

		Meaning
setting	=	where the movie takes place
theme	=	what it's about
period	=	when it takes place
plot	=	story
characters	=	the good guy, bad guy, beautiful young girl
shared iconic images	=	pictures that stay in the mind of audience

3. Why is immigration a "natural subject" for American films?
   Immigration has always been an important part of U.S. history

Section 2

1.
New Term	Definition
the Wild West	a. where? The huge area west of the Mississippi River
	b. when? From 1865 to 1900 or 1910

2. History: What was happening?

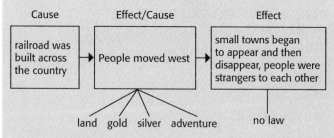

3. Four elements of westerns:
   Simple morality stories, good vs. evil
   A hero, a villain, and a heroine
   Action stories, violence, chase scenes
   Theme—dangers of moving west, or hero saving a town

4. Three iconic images from westerns:
   Cowboy, with hat, alone, riding a horse
   Shootout, two cowboys, one in black hat, one in white
   The land, huge, vast, symbolic of endless possibilities

Section 3

1. History:

Period: The Great Depression

Years: 1929–1940

1. stock market crashed : 1929 (when?)
2. Depression = people poor and hungry
3. Prohibition = a law that made alcohol illegal
   People still drank, lots of organized crime and gangsters
4. W.P.A. (Works Progress Administration): gave jobs to thousands of people and improved the country (post offices, bridges, roads)

2. Film Genres from the Great Depression

Genres	Examples	Iconic Images
1. musical	*42nd Street* *Top Hat* *Singing in the Rain* *A Chorus Line* *Chicago*	Fred Astaire and Ginger Rogers
2. crime drama	*Public Enemy* *Bonnie and Clyde* *The Godfather*	Gangster wearing expensive suit with hat pulled over eye, holding a gun
3. road trip	*It Happened One Night* *The Grapes of Wrath* *Rain Man* *Thelma and Louise*	People in a car on an endless road through the desert

B. Checking Your Notes

○ Go over the directions.
○ Have students read the questions in After Listening Activity A to see if they can answer them from their notes.
○ Have students fill in any missing notes as you play the video or audio program again.

Audio Script

Use the script for Activity A on page 116 of the Teacher's Edition.

ANSWER KEY

Use the outline for Activity A on page 118 of the Teacher's Edition.

After Listening

A. Using Your Notes

○ Go over the directions and the questions.
○ Have students answer the questions and then compare answers with a partner.
○ Call on students to share their answers with the class.

ANSWER KEY

1. a vivid picture that stays in your mind
2. westerns, musicals, crime dramas, road trips
3. western—cowboy on a horse; musical—Fred Astaire and Ginger Rogers; crime drama—gangster in expensive suit with a gun; road trip—people in a car on an endless road in a desert
4. between 1860 and 1910 in vast area west of the Mississippi
5. People moved west for land, gold, silver and adventure
6. 1929–1940
7. People lost their jobs and money. Many people were poor and hungry.

B. Making Inferences

○ Go over the directions.
○ Have students discuss the questions in pairs.
○ Call on students to share their ideas with the class.

ANSWER KEY

The lecturer's style is informal. He asks questions and uses informal language, such as calling his students *guys*.
The shootout symbolizes good vs. evil.

CRITICAL THINKING STRATEGY: Synthesizing

○ Go over the information in the box.
○ Ask questions: *What does it mean to synthesize? As a student, what kinds of information will you have to synthesize?*

TOEFL® iBT Tip

TOEFL iBT Tip 6: The integrated speaking task on the TOEFL iBT tests the ability to read a passage, listen to a lecture related to that passage, and then reply to a question based on the two sources. These reading and listening passages will often present a general principle and a counter example, or a problem and solution.

○ Point out that the critical thinking strategy *Synthesizing* will help students to make connections between what they have heard and what they have read.

○ Remind students to organize their ideas regarding the two sides of an issue before stating an opinion.

C. Making Connections: Synthesizing

○ Go over the directions and the question.
○ Have students discuss the question in pairs or small groups.
○ Call on students to share their ideas with the class.

ANSWER KEY

Both westerns and crime drama have a theme of good vs. evil, with heroes and villains fighting with guns. Walter Hill meant that all his movies have this theme.

Put It All Together

○ Decide if your class will do Project A (if you have students from different countries at your school) or Project B (if everyone in your school is from the same country). Follow the steps for the project you choose.

SPEAKING STRATEGY: Taking a Survey

○ Go over the information in the box.
○ Ask questions: *What is a survey? How can you begin an interview? How should you ask for clarification?*

Project A

○ Go over the information about Project B. Have students read the steps. You can have students work individually or in small groups.

Step 1
○ Have students rent and watch one of the films. Remind students to take notes and to write down anything they think is an iconic image.

Step 2
○ Have students do an Internet search for the film, looking for an analysis, summary or review. Remind students to take notes on what they learn.

Step 3
○ Go over the directions and questions.
○ Have students form groups with classmates who saw different movies to discuss the questions.
○ Call on students to share what they learned with the class.

Project B

○ Go over the information about Project A. Have students read the steps.
○ Contact the teacher of another class ahead of time. Arrange for your students to interview three students in another class.

Step 1
○ Have students interview three students from another class. Remind your students to record the answers in the chart.

Step 2
○ Go over the directions.
○ Have students discuss their surveys in small groups.
○ Call on students to share their ideas with the class.

EXPANSION ACTIVITY: Analysis of Bonnie and Clyde

○ Photocopy and distribute the worksheet *Analysis of Bonnie and Clyde* on page BLM 11.
○ Have students read the passage and answer the questions.
○ Go over the answers with the class.

ANSWER KEY

1. C; 2. C; 3. A; 4. B; 5. A

Unit 3 Vocabulary Workshop

A. Matching
○ Go over the directions.
○ Have students write the correct letters on the lines
   to match the definitions with the words.
○ Go over the answers.

ANSWER KEY
1. g; 2. a; 3. d; 4. i; 5. c; 6. h; 7. f; 8. j; 9. e; 10. b

B. Words in Phrases
○ Go over the directions.
○ Have students write the correct words on the lines
   to complete the phrases.
○ Go over the answers.

ANSWER KEY
1. office; 2. into; 3. target; 4. office; 5. out; 6. into

C. High Frequency Words
○ Go over the directions.
○ Have students write the correct words on the lines.
○ Go over the answers.

ANSWER KEY
1. Slavery; 2. especially; 3. slaves; 4. rice; 5. crops;
6. terrible; 7. dirt; 8. straw; 9. mistakes

Class Outline

I. Undergraduate Students

A. Years

1. Freshman (1st year)

2. Sophomore (2nd)

3. Junior (3rd)

4. Senior (4th)

B. Graduate/receive a degree

1. A.A.

2. B.A.

3. B.S.

II. Graduate School (= grad school)

A. Grad students—in a master's program or Ph.D. program

B. Receive a master's degree (after 2 years)

1. M.A.

2. M.S.

3. M.B.A.

4. M.F.A.

C. Receive a Ph.D.

III. Definitions: College and University

A. Both after high school

B. University

1. Never just 2 years

2. Has a grad school

C. Canada: "I'm in college."/"I'm in university."

D. U.S.: "I'm in college" = college or university

Comparing Advice

Directions: Work with a partner. Compare your chart from Activity A on page 25 with your partner's chart. Write advice that you wrote but your partner didn't in the left section of the Venn diagram below. Write advice you both wrote on the chart in the overlapping section in the middle. Write advice that only your partner wrote in the section on the right.

Your advice   **Advice from both you and your partner**   **Your partner's advice**

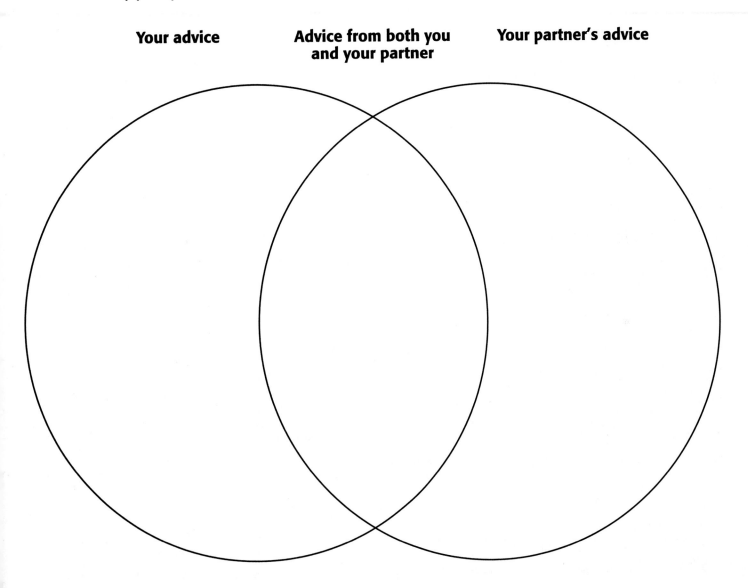

Name: _____   Date: _____

Finding Information on a Website

Directions: Look at the university website. Underlined phrases are links to web pages with more information. Which links would you click on to find the information below? Write the names of the correct links on the lines.

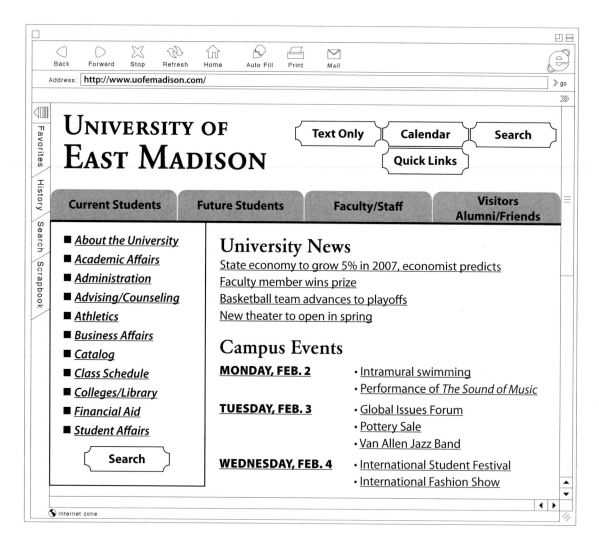

1. types of sports teams _____
2. the name of the university president _____
3. the time that English 111 begins _____
4. how to apply for money for school _____
5. the time the fashion show begins _____
6. the name of the theater _____
7. faculty email _____

Feedback Form

Directions: As you listen to each presentation, complete the form below. Write the presenter's name at the top of the form. For each item, circle 1 (Excellent), 2 (Good), 3 (O.K.), or 4 (Needs Improvement). Then write your own comment of one or two sentences.

Name of presenter: _____

	Excellent	Good	O.K.	Needs Improvement
Easy to understand	1	2	3	4
Volume (loudness)	1	2	3	4
Spoke for 3 minutes	1	2	3	4
Visual design	1	2	3	4
Eye contact	1	2	3	4
Described product	1	2	3	4
Described target market	1	2	3	4

Comment: _____

_____

Feedback Form

Directions: As you listen to each presentation, complete the form below. Write the presenter's name at the top of the form. For each item, circle 1 (Excellent), 2 (Good), 3 (O.K.), or 4 (Needs Improvement). Then write your own comment of one or two sentences.

Name of presenter: _____

	Excellent	Good	O.K.	Needs Improvement
Easy to understand	1	2	3	4
Volume (loudness)	1	2	3	4
Spoke for 3 minutes	1	2	3	4
Visual design	1	2	3	4
Eye contact	1	2	3	4
Described product	1	2	3	4
Described target market	1	2	3	4

Comment: _____

_____

Name: _____ Date: _____

Online Ads

Directions: Read about online advertising. Then answer the questions below. Fill in the correct bubbles.

Although companies have advertised for hundreds of years, online advertising is relatively new. There are several trends in online advertising. There are trends in the choice of shapes, colors, images, layout, promotions, and interactivity—that is, the ability to actively participate in an ad. The designers of online ads use many curved shapes such as circles, arcs, and ovals. The most popular colors in online ads are black, white, orange, and blue. As in print advertising, many companies use photos of happy consumers in ads. Using a human face with a product may allow the consumer to connect more with that product. Most online ads use banners—large ads across the top of a page—with recognizable logos. Perhaps the greatest difference between online advertising and other ads is interactivity. When users can do something with the ad by clicking on icons or playing games, they spend more time with the ad. This means they may become more familiar with and feel more positive about the product.

1. Which shapes are used more often in online advertising?
   - Ⓐ squares
   - Ⓑ circles
   - Ⓒ triangles

2. Which color is more popular in online ads?
   - Ⓐ yellow
   - Ⓑ red
   - Ⓒ blue

3. What is used in both print and online advertising?
   - Ⓐ a happy face
   - Ⓑ arcs
   - Ⓒ banners

4. What is the greatest difference between print ads and online ads?
   - Ⓐ the amount of reading
   - Ⓑ the ability to interact
   - Ⓒ images

5. What is an example of interactivity?
   - Ⓐ logos
   - Ⓑ banners that move
   - Ⓒ clicking on icons

Koko and Michael

Directions: Read about the gorillas Koko and Michael. Then read the statements below and fill in T for *True* or F for *False.*

Koko is a western lowland gorilla who "speaks" both American and Gorilla Sign Language. Dr. Francine "Penny" Patterson started teaching Koko sign language in 1972. Koko has a vocabulary of over 1000 words, and she often begins conversations with humans. She has had to change some of the signs in American Sign Language (ASL) because gorillas' hands are different from human hands. For example, their thumbs are very short. Also, Koko prefers to use some signs instead of others. For example, she knows the sign for *flower,* but she uses the sign for *stink* because she knows that some flowers have a strong smell. Like humans, Koko can express her emotions and create sentences of up to seven words. Koko is so comfortable using sign language that she even signs to herself!

Dr. Patterson has also worked with a gorilla named Michael. Michael died a few years ago. Before he died, Michael had a working sign language vocabulary of 600 words. Although both Koko and Michael could paint, Michael really seemed to enjoy it. He even painted a picture of his pet dog, Apple. Both gorillas could describe their paintings and gave them titles.

1. Koko and Michael are gorillas.   T   F

2. Both can use about 1000 words in ASL.   T   F

3. Scientists created Gorilla Sign Language.   T   F

4. Koko expresses her feelings.   T   F

5. Koko likes painting more than Michael does.   T   F

6. Koko uses sign language only with humans.   T   F

7. Gorillas have shorter thumbs than humans.   T   F

8. Michael painted a picture of an apple for his dog.   T   F

The Okinawan Diet

Directions: Read about nutrition in Okinawa. Then read the sentences below and fill in T for *True* or F for *False.*

Researchers have recently studied the diet of the people of Okinawa, an island in the southern part of Japan, to find out why they lead such long and healthy lives. The average Okinawan lives to age 82 or 83, and there are more people who live to age 100 on Okinawa than anywhere else in the world. Researchers believe one key to such longevity is the diet. Okinawans eat a lot of carbohydrates, especially green vegetables, sweet potatoes, and whole grains. They also eat fish three times a week and many foods that come from the soy bean—these are their most important sources of protein. Their diet includes red meat, but only rarely. Okinawans drink a moderate amount of alcohol, and a lot of tea and water. This diet may help the people of the island avoid many diseases. They have 80% fewer heart attacks than Americans, and many cancers, such as breast and prostate cancers, are rare. Of course, Okinawans also lead healthy lifestyles. They walk a lot and often practice martial arts. Perhaps another key to their long and healthy lives is a practice called *hari hachi bu,* or eating until you are 80% full. Okinawans eat about 1900 calories a day, compared to Americans who eat about 2500. It may be that deciding how much to eat is as important as deciding what to eat.

1. Researchers are studying the causes of disease in Okinawa.   Ⓣ   Ⓕ

2. Okinawans usually live to be 100 years old.   Ⓣ   Ⓕ

3. Okinawans eat a diet that is very rich in carbohydrates.   Ⓣ   Ⓕ

4. Most of their protein comes from red meat.   Ⓣ   Ⓕ

5. There is less heart disease on Okinawa than in the U.S.   Ⓣ   Ⓕ

6. Okinawans get a lot of exercise.   Ⓣ   Ⓕ

7. People on Okinawa eat as much as most Americans.   Ⓣ   Ⓕ

8. *Hari hachi bu* means "eat healthy."   Ⓣ   Ⓕ

9. Okinawans drink a lot of alcohol.   Ⓣ   Ⓕ

10. Cancer is rare in the U.S.   Ⓣ   Ⓕ

Name: _____ **Date:** _____

Comparing Chapter Sections

Directions: Look back at the lecture outline on pages 167–168 and your notes on the radio interview in Part 4. Write information that was only in Part 4 of the chapter in the left section of the Venn diagram below. Write information that you found in both Part 4 and Part 5 in the overlapping center section. Write information that was only in Part 5 in the section on the right.

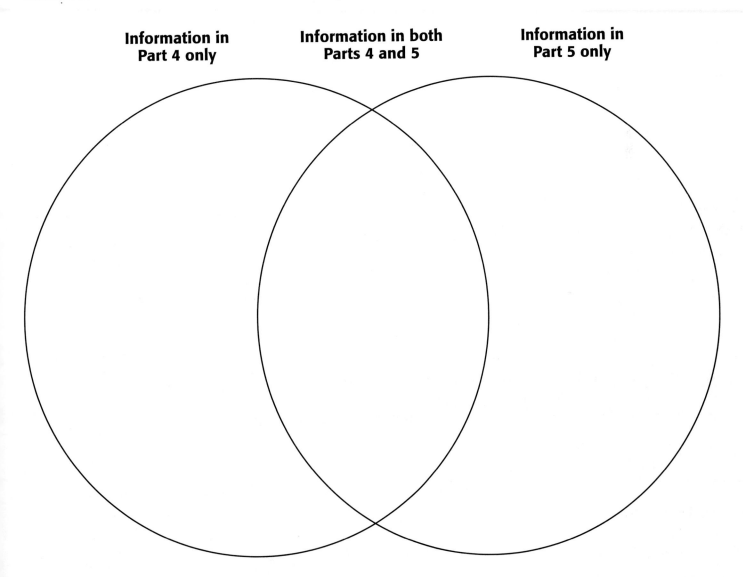

Information in Part 4 only   **Information in both Parts 4 and 5**   **Information in Part 5 only**

After you complete the Venn diagram, share your answers in small groups.

Feedback Form

Directions: As you listen to each presentation, complete the form below. Write the presenter's name at the top of the form. For each item, circle 1 (Excellent), 2 (Good), 3 (O.K.), or 4 (Needs Improvement). Then write your own comment of one or two sentences.

Name of presenter: _____

	Excellent	Good	O.K.	Needs Improvement
Easy to understand	1	2	3	4
Volume (loudness)	1	2	3	4
Spoke for 3 minutes	1	2	3	4
Visual design	1	2	3	4
Eye contact	1	2	3	4
Described product	1	2	3	4
Described target market	1	2	3	4

Comment: _____

_____

Feedback Form

Directions: As you listen to each presentation, complete the form below. Write the presenter's name at the top of the form. For each item, circle 1 (Excellent), 2 (Good), 3 (O.K.), or 4 (Needs Improvement). Then write your own comment of one or two sentences.

Name of presenter: _____

	Excellent	Good	O.K.	Needs Improvement
Easy to understand	1	2	3	4
Volume (loudness)	1	2	3	4
Spoke for 3 minutes	1	2	3	4
Visual design	1	2	3	4
Eye contact	1	2	3	4
Described product	1	2	3	4
Described target market	1	2	3	4

Comment: _____

_____

Name: _____ Date: _____

Harriet Tubman

Directions: Read about Harriet Tubman's life. Then read the questions below and write the correct answers on the lines.

Harriet Tubman was the most famous of the "conductors" on the Underground Railroad. She was born around 1820 to slaves in Maryland. Her parents were from the Ashanti tribe in Africa. Harriet did housework when she was a little girl, but in her teens she became a field hand, or farm worker. Once, she tried to protect another slave from an overseer—one of the men who supervised the slaves. The overseer hit Harriet in the head with a heavy piece of metal. For the rest of her life, she sometimes had blackouts—suddenly became unconscious—as a result of this injury. She married John Tubman, a free black, in 1845. In 1849, Harriet was afraid that she would be sold, so she escaped to Pennsylvania with the help of a friendly white woman. But Harriet did not remain in the safety of the North. She returned to help her family members escape: first her sisters, then her brothers, and finally her 70-year-old parents. By then, she and her husband had separated. He didn't follow Harriet north. Over the next 10 years, Harriet made 19 more trips south, and she freed more than 300 slaves. Her last journey on the Underground Railroad was in 1860. The next year, the Civil War began. During the war, Harriet became a soldier, a nurse, and a spy for the North. In 1870, Harriet married Nelson Davis, a northern soldier who was more than 20 years younger than her. She died in 1913.

1. Where was Harriet Tubman born? _____

2. Why did she escape? _____

3. How many slaves did she help to free? _____

4. Why did she have blackouts? _____

5. What did Harriet do during the Civil War? _____

Directions: Complete the timeline. Write events from the paragraph above next to the years when they occurred.

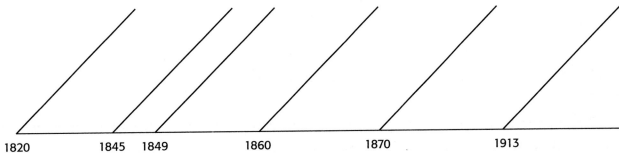

1820   1845 1849   1860   1870   1913

Analysis of Bonnie and Clyde

Directions: Read about an American gangster movie. Then answer the questions below. Fill in the correct bubbles.

Bonnie and Clyde is a movie in the gangster genre about a man and a woman who were partners in crime during the Great Depression—a period of economic troubles in the 1930s. The characters were real people, and they have become famous symbols of violent but romantic rebellion.

The movie is set in Texas and Oklahoma, part of America's farming country. At the time of the story, there had been no rain for several years. The crops failed, and the fields changed into dust and blew away. People began to call that region "The Dust Bowl." Many farmers lost their farms and their way of making a living.

In the movie, Clyde Barrow and Bonnie Parker meet when he is trying to steal her mother's car. Within minutes, he has robbed a store, and they escape in another stolen car. This begins their crime spree—that is, committing many crimes in a short time. The movie ends in a gun battle by the side of a highway. Both Bonnie and Clyde die bloodily, shot by many bullets.

Living in the Dust Bowl, Clyde believes that crime is the only way to escape poverty and "be somebody"—be important and have self-respect. Although they hate authority, Bonnie and Clyde are loyal to each other and to their friends.

Arthur Penn directed *Bonnie and Clyde* during the 1960s, a time when many young people in the United States had strong anti-authority feelings, and so some viewers admired the wild behavior of the criminal pair. The movie was criticized for its violence, but it also won many awards.

1. What is the main idea of this passage?
   - Ⓐ *Bonnie and Clyde* is a famous film that won many awards.
   - Ⓑ *Bonnie and Clyde* is set in Texas and Oklahoma during the Depression.
   - Ⓒ *Bonnie and Clyde* uses the gangster genre to show the theme of rebellion.

2. Who was the director of *Bonnie and Clyde*?
   - Ⓐ Clyde Barrow
   - Ⓑ Bonnie Parker
   - Ⓒ Arthur Penn

3. When was the movie made?
   - Ⓐ the 1960s
   - Ⓑ the 1930s
   - Ⓒ the 1860s

4. How do the two main characters meet?
   - Ⓐ They work in a bank together.
   - Ⓑ He tries to steal her mother's car.
   - Ⓒ He robs a store and kidnaps her.

5. Based on the definition of *crime spree,* what is the most likely meaning for the phrase *shopping spree?*
   - Ⓐ Buying many things in a short time.
   - Ⓑ Robbing a store.
   - Ⓒ Shopping for a car.

Name: _____ Date: _____ Score: _____

A. Language Function: Asking for/Following Directions

Directions: Listen to the people giving directions. As you listen, look at the map below. Follow the directions from the place marked *You are here.* Write the letters of the correct places on the lines.

_____ **1.** library

_____ **2.** Taylor Gym

_____ **3.** copy center

_____ **4.** bookstore

_____ **5.** Science and Technology

YOU ARE
HERE
↓

Student Union

A

Wrigley
Administration
Building

B

University Avenue

Main Street

Parker Road

C

Barnard
Hall

D

E

B. Intonation: Understanding Interjections

Directions: Listen to the conversations. What does the second person mean? Check (✔) the correct box.

	Yes.	No.	You're welcome.	Pardon?/What?	There's a problem.
1.	☐	☐	☐	☐	☐
2.	☐	☐	☐	☐	☐
3.	☐	☐	☐	☐	☐
4.	☐	☐	☐	☐	☐
5.	☐	☐	☐	☐	☐

🎧 C. Pronunciation: /θ/ vs. /s/

Directions: Listen and circle the word that you hear.

1. worth   worse
2. tenth   tense
3. things   sings

4. thank   sank
5. forth   force

🎧 D. Listening Comprehension

Directions: Read the questions. Then listen to the orientation and fill in the bubbles of the correct answers.

1. Where can students get help with registering for classes?
   - Ⓐ Academic Learning Center
   - Ⓑ International Student Office
   - Ⓒ Library

2. What does the language lab have for ESL students?
   - Ⓐ a list of classes
   - Ⓑ tutors
   - Ⓒ materials for classes

3. How can students learn about the library?
   - Ⓐ take a tour
   - Ⓑ talk to a tutor
   - Ⓒ take an online tutorial

4. What is the most important thing for new ESL students to do?
   - Ⓐ register for classes
   - Ⓑ get to know the college culture
   - Ⓒ study hard

🎧 E. Vocabulary

Directions: Listen to sentences from the lecture. Write the correct words from the box on the lines.

experiment	key	roughly	tutors

1. This year, we have _____ 500 ESL students enrolled.

2. Okay, so in your first weeks, several resources are going to be _____ to helping you get off to a good start.

3. The ALC has a computer lab, _____, and lots of materials that can help you get organized.

4. Now is a good time to _____, try new subjects, different activities.

Name: _____ **Date:** _____ **Score:** _____

🎧 A. Intonation: *Wh–* Questions

Directions: Listen to the questions. Circle *Correct* if the intonation is correct, and *Incorrect* if it is incorrect.

1.   Correct   Incorrect
2.   Correct   Incorrect
3.   Correct   Incorrect
4.   Correct   Incorrect
5.   Correct   Incorrect

🎧 B. Language Function: Greeting and Responding to Greetings

Directions: Listen to the greetings. Circle the best response.

1.   Fine.   Not much.
2.   Fine.   Not much.
3.   Fine.   Not much.
4.   Fine.   Not much.
5.   Fine.   Not much.

🎧 C. Pronunciation: Reduced Forms of Words

Directions: Listen to the conversation. You'll hear the reduced forms of some words. Write the long forms on the lines.

1. **A:** Hey, Jill. _____ going?

2. **B:** Good. _____ with you?

3. **A:** Not much. I just started classes. How _____?

4. **B:** I'm not taking _____ classes this year.

5. **A:** I sure am. I _____ if I can handle so many.

🎧 D. Listening Comprehension

Directions: Read the questions. Then listen to the lecture and fill in the bubbles of the correct answers.

1. What is the main idea?
   - Ⓐ global marketing ideas
   - Ⓑ global marketing mistakes
   - Ⓒ global marketing success stories

2. Which of the following was a problem for Snapple?
   - Ⓐ language   Ⓑ attitudes   Ⓒ pictures on package

3. What was the problem for American Airlines in trying to advertise its new leather seats?
   - Ⓐ language   Ⓑ product research Ⓒ financial resources

4. What is one way the Asian market differs from the American market?
   - Ⓐ Asian men shave less often.
   - Ⓑ Not all Asians read, so companies put pictures of the ingredients on the package.
   - Ⓒ Women are not usually shown without a veil.

5. Which of the following companies sells camera supplies?
   - Ⓐ Snapple   Ⓑ Gerber   Ⓒ Fuji

🎧 E. Vocabulary

Directions: Listen to sentences from the lecture. Write the correct words and phrases from the box on the lines.

demand	marketing	perfected	point-of-purchase displays	pulp

1. I'd just like to review some of the issues we've talked about related to global

   _____.

2. The company had great _____, but a terrible product image for the Japanese.

3. They didn't try to change the attitude of the Japanese, to convince them that
   _____ added quality.

4. Clearly, there would be less _____ for the product.

5. The airlines hadn't _____ its message yet.

Name: _____ **Date:** _____ **Score:** _____

A. Intonation: Statements and Questions

Directions: Listen to the sentences. Are they statements or questions? Circle *Statement* or *Question.*

1. Statement   Question

2. Statement   Question

3. Statement   Question

4. Statement   Question

5. Statement   Question

B. Language Function: Responding to a Negative Question

Directions: Listen to the conversations. Is the second speaker agreeing or disagreeing with the negative question? Circle *Agree* or *Disagree.*

1. Agree   Disagree

2. Agree   Disagree

3. Agree   Disagree

4. Agree   Disagree

5. Agree   Disagree

C. Pronunciation: Reduced Forms of Words

Directions: Listen to the conversation. You'll hear the reduced form of some words. Write the long forms of the words on the lines.

1. A: Are you _____ go to Diana's party on Friday?

2. B: I _____. Are you?

3. A: Maybe. I'll call _____ later and get the details.

4. B: I've _____ get someone to work for me if I decide to go.

5. A: Better hurry. You're almost _____ time. The party is in two days.

⌒ D. Listening Comprehension

Directions: Read the questions. Then listen to the lecture and fill in the bubbles of the correct answers.

1. What is the main idea?
   - Ⓐ Some animals can use language in an advanced way.
   - Ⓑ Chimpanzees have an understanding of "self."
   - Ⓒ Research suggests that chimps and apes may be able to "think" in some ways.
2. According to the professor, what are three different ways that animals may think?
   - Ⓐ using tools, following directions, using language
   - Ⓑ using language, understanding self, and having a concept of a mind
   - Ⓒ recognizing self, understanding research, using language
3. Megan looked in a mirror and touched her head. What does this suggest?
   - Ⓐ She was making the sign for thinking.
   - Ⓑ She was telling the trainer her head hurt.
   - Ⓒ She saw a mark on the image in the mirror in that spot.
4. Who knows 1000 words in sign language?
   - Ⓐ Washoe Ⓑ Koko Ⓒ Sheba
5. What animals does the professor talk about?
   - Ⓐ chimps and parrots Ⓑ dogs and apes Ⓒ chimps and gorillas

⌒ E. Vocabulary

Directions: Listen to sentences from the lecture. Write the correct words from the box on the lines.

capacity	distinguishes	novel	species	unconscious

1. She not only uses words she has been taught, she can create words to talk about a _____ idea.
2. Second, do animals have a _____ for self-awareness?
3. In one study, researchers put a mark on a chimpanzee's head while she was _____.
4. In other words, she _____ between the trainer who knows and the trainer who just guesses about the food.
5. Such research may one day show us that animals, at least those _____ similar to us, do think in ways that are similar to humans.

Name: _____ **Date:** _____ **Score:** _____

⌒ A. Language Function: Asking for More Information and Examples

Directions: Listen to the conversations. Speaker A makes a statement. Speaker B asks a question. Decide if Speaker B is asking informal or formal questions. Circle *Informal* or *Formal*.

1. Informal   Formal

2. Informal   Formal

3. Informal   Formal

4. Informal   Formal

5. Informal   Formal

⌒ B. Language Function: Giving Reasons or Examples

Directions: Listen to the questions. Fill in the bubbles of the best responses.

1. Ⓐ Because it's good for me.   Ⓑ like green leafy vegetables
2. Ⓐ One reason is it's low in fat.   Ⓑ salmon and other fatty fish
3. Ⓐ Because it's spicy.   Ⓑ vitamin A and D
4. Ⓐ It helps with weight loss.   Ⓑ fruits and vegetables
5. Ⓐ Because it tasts good.   Ⓑ Spinach is a good example.

⌒ C. Pronunciation: Reduced Forms of Words

Directions: Listen to the conversation. You'll hear the reduced forms of some words. Write the long forms on the lines.

1. **A:** _____ say you went this morning?

2. **B:** To the doctor's. _____ ask?

3. **A:** I forgot, and Mr. Parker asked about you. _____ go again?

4. **B:** I haven't been sleeping very well. _____ tell Mr. Parker?

5. **A:** Well, I said you had an appointment. _____ get back?

🎧 D. Listening Comprehension

Directions: Read the questions. Then listen to the lecture and fill in the bubbles of the correct answers.

1. What is the topic?
   - Ⓐ nutrition
   - Ⓑ Okinawa
   - Ⓒ the Mediterranean diet

2. What are antioxidants?
   - Ⓐ bad fats
   - Ⓑ good fats
   - Ⓒ chemicals that get rid of bad substances

3. What do Okinawans eat a lot?
   - Ⓐ tomatoes
   - Ⓑ pasta
   - Ⓒ sweet potatoes

4. What is a healthy aspect of the Okinawan diet?
   - Ⓐ They walk a lot.
   - Ⓑ They eat a lot of antioxidants.
   - Ⓒ They don't eat very many calories.

5. What is true about the Mediterranean diet?
   - Ⓐ It's low in all fats.
   - Ⓑ It's high in heart-healthy fats.
   - Ⓒ It's low in calories.

🎧 E. Vocabulary

Directions: Listen to sentences from the lecture. Write the correct words and phrases from the box on the lines.

complex carbohydrates	cuisine	in abundance	life expectancy	promoting

1. We've talked about the basics of nutrition, and the importance of all the nutrients in

   _____ good health.

2. We need a lot of _____ such as whole grains and vegetables that contain a lot of vitamins.

3. What was so healthy about that _____?

4. It had fruits and vegetables _____.

5. The people on Okinawa have a longer _____ on average than most people in the world.

Name: _____ **Date:** _____ **Score:** _____

🎧 A. Language Function: Introducing Yourself and Responding to an Introduction

Directions: Listen to the conversations. Write the words that you hear on the lines.

1. **A:** Hi, John. I'm Kathy. _____.

   B: Hi. Kathy. _____?

2. **A:** Hello, Greg. _____. I'm Robert.

   B: Oh, hi, Robert. _____.

3. **A:** Hi, Cynthia. I'm Linda. _____.

🎧 B. Pronunciation: /I/ vs. /i/

Directions: Listen to the following words. Circle the word that you hear.

1.	bit	beat
2.	pick	peek
3.	his	he's
4.	live	leave
5.	it	eat

C. Which Word Doesn't Belong?

Directions: In each row, cross out the word or phrase without a connection to the other two.

1.	field hand	personal	first-hand
2.	enduring	perseverance	surprising
3.	denounced	supported	criticized
4.	depended on	required	arrested
5.	political job	public office	work area

⌒ D. Listening Comprehension

Directions: Read the questions. Then listen to the interview and fill in the bubbles of the correct answers.

1. What is the main idea?
   - ⓐ Songs and quilts gave coded messages about the Underground Railroad.
   - ⓑ Ruth Givens works at the African-American Cultural Center.
   - ⓒ There are two types of coded songs.

2. What is a quilt?
   - ⓐ a religious song　　　ⓑ a type of blanket　　　ⓒ an exhibit at a museum

3. What kind of information was given in both spirituals and in quilts?
   - ⓐ when to leave　　　ⓑ what stars to follow　　　ⓒ what routes to use

4. How did slaves communicate with quilts?
   - ⓐ They put them in the window.
   - ⓑ They sang them in the fields.
   - ⓒ They put them on the beds.

5. Who are the two speakers?
   - ⓐ a professor and a student
   - ⓑ a radio host and guest
   - ⓒ a visitor to the museum and a guide

⌒ E. Vocabulary

Directions: Listen to sentences from the interview. Write the correct words and phrases from the box on the lines.

crops	find their way	role	win their freedom

1. Well, spirituals, as you know, are the religious songs that the slaves used to sing in the fields as they picked the _____.

2. For example, *Follow the Drinking Gourd* told slaves to follow the Big Dipper constellation as they headed north to _____.

3. Now how did quilts play a _____ in the Underground Railroad?

4. So, slaves could hang particular quilts in the windowsill to help escaping slaves _____ north.

Name: _____ **Date:** _____ **Score:** _____

🎧 A. Pronunciation: Verbs Ending in *-ed*

Directions: Listen to each past tense verb. Is the ending pronounced /t/, /d/, or /ɪd/? Use both your listening ability and the three rules from the box on page 185 to help you decide. Check (✔) the correct pronunciation. You'll hear each verb two times.

	/t/	/d/	/ɪd/
1. turned	_____	_____	_____
2. watched	_____	_____	_____
3. laughed	_____	_____	_____
4. pointed	_____	_____	_____
5. studied	_____	_____	_____
6. appreciated	_____	_____	_____
7. joked	_____	_____	_____
8. agreed	_____	_____	_____
9. killed	_____	_____	_____
10. passed	_____	_____	_____

🎧 B. Intonation: Showing Disagreement with Intonation

Directions: Listen to the conversations. Pay attention to the second person's intonation. Does this person truly agree? If so, circle *Agree.* Or do you think that this person will say "but . . . " and then disagree? If so, circle *Disagree.*

1.	Agree	Disagree
2.	Agree	Disagree
3.	Agree	Disagree
4.	Agree	Disagree
5.	Agree	Disagree

🎧 C. Listening Comprehension

Directions: Read the questions. Then listen to the lecture and fill in the bubbles of the correct answers.

1. What is the main idea?
   - Ⓐ There are several genres in film, including musicals, westerns, and gangster films.
   - Ⓑ Films, including musicals, became popular during the Great Depression.
   - Ⓒ One film genre, the musical, started in the 1920s and continues to today.

2. Why were musicals popular in the 1930s?
   - Ⓐ They were cheaper than other movies.
   - Ⓑ They offered an escape from the hard times.
   - Ⓒ Everyone liked to sing.

3. Who was a popular child star during the 1930s?
   - Ⓐ Shirley Temple   Ⓑ Al Jolson   Ⓒ Fred Astaire

4. When was *The Sound of Music* made?
   - Ⓐ 1930s   Ⓑ 1940s   Ⓒ 1960s

5. What type of film is often a musical today?
   - Ⓐ westerns   Ⓑ animated films   Ⓒ gangster movies

🎧 D. Vocabulary

Directions: Listen to sentences from the lecture. Write the correct words from the box on the lines.

box office	comeback	genre	plot	romanticized

1. Today, I'd like to look at one _____ we haven't talked about too much— the American musical.

2. Musicals, as you know, combine song and dance routines to help move the _____ along and tell the story.

3. After a while, however, audiences tired of the musical's _____ stories.

4. Musicals continued to be popular at the _____ during the 1940s and 1950s.

5. Through animated movies, like the Disney hits *Beauty and the Beast*, *Aladdin*, and *The Little Mermaid*, the musical made a _____ as children's entertainment.

Chapter 1 Test Audio Script

A.

1. A: Excuse me. Can you tell me where the library is?
B: Sure. Go one block and turn left on Main Street. Go another block, and you'll see the library on your left, on the corner of Main and Parker.
2. A: Excuse me. How can I get to Taylor Gym?
B: Uh, yeah. Go one block to Main Street. Turn left and go two blocks. Taylor Gym is on the right.
3. A: Excuse me. Could you tell me where I can find a copy center?
B: Yeah. Go one block and turn right. It's the little building next to the Student Union.
4. A: Excuse me. Do you know where the bookstore is?
B: Yes. It's one block down, across from the Student Union, on Main Street.
5. A: Excuse me. Can you tell me how to get to the Science and Technology building?
B: Sure. Go one block, turn left on Main. It'll be on your right, next to Barnard Hall.

B.

1. A: I heard there's a test tomorrow.
B: Uh-oh.
2. A: Thanks for the book.
B: Uh-huh.
3. A: We're meeting in 10 minutes.
B: Huh?
4. A: She's a great teacher.
B: Uh-huh.
5. A: Is this Biology 101?
B: Uh-uh.

C.

1. worse
2. tenth
3. sings
4. sank
5. forth

D.

Welcome to the orientation for new English as a Second Language students. First of all, I'd like to welcome you to Valley College. This year, we have roughly 500 ESL students enrolled. That's the largest number since we began accepting ESL students 20 years ago. Today, I'm going to give you an overview of the campus resources that may help you adjust to the school, and then I want to talk a little bit about what you can do to make sure you succeed here.

O.K., so in your first weeks, several resources are going to be key to helping you get off to a good start. First of all, you need to know how to find the International Student Office. We're located in 223 Harper Hall, as most of you already know. What do we do? Well, we'll help you figure out what classes you need to take, and then help you through the registration process. We can also help you add or drop classes during the first two weeks of school. Another important resource is the Academic Learning Center. The ALC has a computer lab, tutors, and a lot of materials that can help you get organized. The Language Lab on the third floor of Baker Hall is also a great resource. The staff can help you with materials for your classes. You should also become familiar with the library in the first few weeks. There are many online and print resources available to you. You can even take an online tutorial on how to use the library. We'll make sure you have campus maps and a list of other helpful places, such as the bookstore, copy center, and student parking lots.

Before we break into smaller groups, I want to talk a little bit about getting to know the college culture. That's probably the most important thing for you to do, but sometimes it's the hardest. American colleges and universities may be a little different from universities in other countries. You have to get involved right away. Many students benefit from study groups. You have to meet your classmates if you want to be part of a group. You can introduce yourself in classes or become involved in campus activities. The Student Life Center has a list of clubs, sports, and other activities. Talk to your instructors. Ask questions. The more you know about your professors, the more you'll know what to expect in their classes. Explore the campus. Walk around and see where students study, relax, and socialize. Now is the perfect time to experiment, try new subjects, different activities. You're college students—enjoy it!

E.

1. This year, we have roughly 500 ESL students enrolled.
2. O.K., so in your first weeks, several resources are going to be key to helping you get off to a good start.
3. The ALC has a computer lab, tutors, and lots of materials that can help you get organized.
4. Now is the perfect time to experiment, try new subjects, different activities.

Chapter 2 Test Audio Script

A.

1. What have you been doing lately? [*Falling intonation*]
2. Where did you buy that dress? [*Rising intonation*]
3. How are you feeling? [*Falling intonation*]
4. Who is meeting you here? [*Falling intonation*]
5. Why are you late? [*Rising intonation*]

B.

1. What's up?
2. How's it going?
3. What have you been up to?
4. How are things with you?
5. What's new with you?

C.

1. **A:** Hey, Jill. Howzit going?
2. **B:** Good. Whasup with you?
3. **A:** Not much. I just started classes. How boutchu?
4. **B:** I'm not taking a lotta classes this term.
5. **A:** I sure am. I dunno if I can handle so many.

D.

I'd just like to review some of the issues we've talked about related to global marketing. We've looked at the case of Snapple and the mistakes that were made in trying to market their drinks in Japan. What were some of those mistakes? The company had great point-of-purchase displays, but a terrible product image for the Japanese. They didn't do the product research that would have told them that, at that time, the Japanese liked purity, not pulp. They didn't try to change the attitude of the Japanese, to convince them that pulp added quality. And Snapple didn't have the financial resources to develop a separate product line for the Japanese market.

O.K. good. So what other marketing mistakes have we talked about? That's right, we've got other problems related to culture, especially language. Things don't always translate properly. American Airlines wanted to call attention to its new leather seats in first class. However, the company's slogan "fly in leather" in Mexico translated as "fly naked,"—the airline hadn't perfected its message yet.

These cultural problems can extend to the packaging. Gerber Baby Foods put a picture of a smiling baby on the jar of baby food, but in Africa, companies put a picture of what's in the product on the package. You can imagine how surprised Africans were to see a baby on the package! Another company wanted to sell razors in Asia. They found out that Asians shave much less often than Americans do, only five or six times a month in some countries. Clearly, there would be less demand for the product. Fujifilm wanted to sell its film for cameras in Saudi Arabia. The company planned to show smiling faces of men, women, and children. Well, in many Arabic countries, it's not proper to show women without their veils—cloth that covers their hair and part of their face. The original marketing idea would not work in Arabic countries.

E.

1. I'd just like to review some of the issues we've talked about related to global marketing.
2. The company had great point-of-purchase displays, but a terrible product image for the Japanese.
3. They didn't try to change the attitude of the Japanese, to convince them that pulp added quality.
4. Clearly, there would be less demand for the product.
5. The airline hadn't perfected its message yet.

Chapter 3 Test Audio Script

A.

1. He's coming at 3:00?
2. I'm speaking next.
3. The bus is late.
4. She's in New York?
5. You forgot we have a test?

B.

1. **A:** You didn't lock the car?
   B: Yes, I did.
2. **A:** You don't like Chinese food?
   B: No, I don't.
3. **A:** Jake wasn't in class today?
   B: Yes, he was.
4. **A:** We didn't have a test?
   B: No, we didn't. The T.A. moved it to Thursday.
5. **A:** Michelle can't swim?
   B: No, she can't. She never learned.

C.

1. A: Are you gonna go to Diana's party on Friday?
2. B: I dunno. Are you?
3. A: Maybe. I'll call 'er later and get the details.
4. B: I gotta get someone to work for me if I decide to go.
5. A: Better hurry. You're almost outta time. The party is in two days.

D.

Do animals think? Let's take a look at some of our closest relatives, the apes and chimpanzees, to see what they can tell us about the ability of animals to think. We're going to talk about three things: the ability to use language, self-awareness, and the understanding of "mind." First, language. Washoe is a chimpanzee that was taught to use American Sign Language, or ASL. She not only uses words she has been taught, she can create words to talk about a novel idea. For example, she had never seen a swan, but immediately signed "waterbird" when she saw one for the first time. Koko, a gorilla, knows more than 1000 words in ASL and can create sentences of up to seven words.

Second, do animals have a capacity for self-awareness? One thing that may make people different from animals is their ability to recognize "self," to know that they are individuals, separate from others. It's unclear if animals have any awareness of self, but some studies have been done. Researchers have worked with chimpanzees to learn more about this. In one study, researchers put a mark on a chimpanzee's head while she was unconscious. After the chimp woke up, the researchers showed her a mirror. When the chimp saw the mark on the mirror, she touched the same spot on her head, suggesting that she knew she was looking at herself.

Last is the issue of whether animals understand there is something like a mind. In another experiment with a chimpanzee, this one called Sheba, researchers tried to find out if Sheba had such a concept. The experiment involved two trainers. Sheba saw one trainer put food in a cup, but Sheba couldn't see which cup. Then another trainer came in. The trainers each point to a different cup to indicate there is food in it. Sheba picks the cup that the first trainer is pointing to.

This suggests that she has an idea that the first trainer knows where the food is. In other words, she distinguishes between the trainer who knows and the trainer who just guesses about the food. Although these studies are still in the beginning stages, such research may one day show us that animals, at least those species similar to us, do think in ways that are similar to humans.

E.

1. She not only uses words she has been taught, she can create words to talk about a novel idea.
2. Second, do animals have a capacity for self-awareness?
3. In one study, researchers put a mark on a chimpanzee's head while she was unconscious.
4. In other words, she distinguishes between the trainer who knows and the trainer who just guesses about the food.
5. Such research may one day show us that animals, at least those species similar to us, do think in ways that are similar to humans.

Chapter 4 Test Audio Script

A.

1. A: I really like Mexican food.
   B: How come?
2. A: A lot of Italian food is really good for you.
   B: Like what?
3. A: Some kinds of fat are actually healthy.
   B: Could you give me an example?
4. A: Eating fish is very healthy.
   B: In what way is fish very healthy?
5. A: Some fast food restaurants offer healthy choices.
   B: Such as?

B.

1. How come?
2. Such as what?
3. Why do you say that?
4. In what way?
5. Like what?

C.

1. A: Whereja say you went this morning?

2. B: To the doctor's. Whydya ask?

3. A: I forgot, and Mr. Parker asked about you. Whyja go again?

4. B: I haven't been sleeping very well. Whaja tell Mr. Parker?

5. A: Well, I said you had an appointment. Whenja get back?

D.

O.K., today I want to talk about how nutrition can affect your long-term health, and even how long you live. We've talked about the basics of nutrition, and the importance of all the nutrients—carbohydrates, fats, proteins, vitamins, minerals, and water—in promoting good health. Remember that while all nutrients are important, we need them in different amounts. For example, we only need a little fat, and of the right kind, while we need a lot of complex carbohydrates such as whole grains and vegetables that contain a lot of vitamins.

We talked yesterday about the Mediterranean diet. What was so healthy about that cuisine? It had fruits and vegetables in abundance, especially green leafy vegetables and tomatoes, foods that are rich in special chemicals called antioxidants. These antioxidants help the body get rid of bad substances that make us less healthy. Also, the Mediterranean diet was rich in good fats, the ones that keep our hearts healthy, and very low in the bad fats that cause heart disease.

We looked at the Chinese diet, and how it is relatively healthy if you watch the sodium content. I'd like to talk a little bit about a special Asian diet, the diet on the island of Okinawa. Okinawa is an island that's part of Japan. The people on Okinawa have a longer life expectancy on average than most people in the world, and there are a greater percentage of people over 100 years of age than anywhere else. Why? Okinawans eat a lot of seafood, soybeans, sweet potatoes, and other vegetables. They walk a lot. And perhaps even more important, they actually restrict calories. They eat much less each day than the average American. In fact, some people recommend that simply cutting the amount that we eat every day would make us healthier. Not to lose weight, but to take advantage of the benefits that come from eating less than you might think you need. The important thing though, is that you have to make sure you are getting enough nutrients.

E.

1. We've talked about the basics of nutrition, and the importance of all the nutrients—carbohydrates, fats, proteins, vitamins, minerals, and water—in promoting good health.

2. We need a lot of complex carbohydrates such as whole grains and vegetables that contain a lot of vitamins.

3. What was so healthy about that cuisine?

4. It had fruits and vegetables in abundance.

5. The people on Okinawa have a longer life expectancy on average than most people in the world.

Chapter 5 Test Audio Script

A.

1. A: Hi, John. I'm Kathy. We met last week.

B: Hi, Kathy. How have you been?

2. A: Hello, Greg. You may not recognize me. I'm Robert.

B: Oh, hi, Robert. Nice to see you again.

3. A: Hi, Cynthia. I'm Linda. I'm in your English class.

B.

1. beat

2. pick

3. he's

4. leave

5. it

D.

Host: I'm Mark Todd, and I'd like to welcome our guest today, Dr. Ruth Givens from the African-American Cultural Center. She's going to tell us a little bit about some of the displays at the cultural center related to the Underground Railroad. Welcome, Dr. Givens.

Ruth: Thanks, Mark. I'm really glad to be here. Please call me Ruth.

Host: Ruth, tell us a little bit about the Underground Railroad. What exactly is it?

Ruth: Well, the Underground Railroad was a network of people and safe houses on a route from the South to the North, that helped African Americans escape slavery. It was especially active in the decade before the Civil War.

Host: And what kind of exhibits do you have at the cultural center that relate to the Underground Railroad?

Ruth: Well, we're really excited because we have both an exhibit about spirituals and one about quilts—both were key tools in communicating about the railroad to the escaping slaves.

Host: Sounds fascinating. How did that work?

Ruth: Well, spirituals, as you know, are the religious songs that the slaves used to sing in the fields as they picked the crops. The spirituals could be codes that gave slaves information. Two common types of codes were signal songs and map songs. Signal songs communicated that an event, such as an escape, was about to happen. Map songs actually gave information about points along the route. For example, "Follow the Drinking Gourd" told slaves to follow the Big Dipper constellation as they headed north to win their freedom.

Host: Now, how did quilts play a role in the Underground Railroad?

Ruth: The evidence for codes in quilts is a little less clear, but many historians think that slaves also used quilts to give information. Quilts were often made by the slaves themselves, so they could sew patterns into the blankets. These patterns told other slaves about routes to use and distances between the stops on the Underground Railroad. It was common to take quilts off the bed and hang them out the window to air. So, slaves could hang particular quilts in the windowsill to help escaping slaves find their way north.

E.

1. Well, spirituals, as you know, are the religious songs that the slaves used to sing in the fields as they picked the crops.
2. For example, "Follow the Drinking Gourd" told slaves to follow the Big Dipper constellation as they headed north to win their freedom.
3. Now, how did quilts play a role in the Underground Railroad?
4. So, slaves could hang particular quilts in the windowsill to help escaping slaves find their way north.

Chapter 6 Test Audio Script

A.

1. turned
2. watched
3. laughed
4. pointed
5. studied
6. appreciated
7. joked
8. agreed
9. killed
10. passed

B.

1. **A:** Today's best movies are not made in Hollywood
   B: True. [*Agrees*]
2. **A:** Most films have some elements of more than one genre.
   B: You have a point. [*Agrees*]
3. **A:** Watching violent movies makes children misbehave.
   B: I see your point . . . [*Disagrees*]
4. **A:** People don't want to think too much when they go to see a movie.
   B: That's true . . . [*Disagrees*]
5. **A:** Musicals are too unrealistic to take seriously.
   B: Yeah . . . [*Disagrees*]

C.

Today I'd like to look at one genre we haven't talked about too much—the American musical. The musical was perhaps the last film genre to come on the scene. Remember that in the early history of film, movies were silent. The musical couldn't exist until movies could combine sound with pictures. So we saw the first musicals really during the 1920s, and they became very popular during the Great Depression. Musicals, as you know, combine song and dance to help move the plot along and tell the story. The actors themselves are usually the ones who sing, rather than having a song in the background sung by another artist. Al Jolson was perhaps the earliest star of the musical genre. The 1930s were the beginning of the Golden Age of the Musical, and many composers, singers, and musicians made their way out to Hollywood and a new career. One reason for the popularity of musicals was their positive message during a pretty difficult time for most people. They offered pure escape to those who could afford a ticket. After a while, however, audiences tired of the musical's romanticized stories, and preferred the westerns and gangster films of that time. The Broadway dance director, Busby Berkeley, brought some excitement back to the musical with his very elaborate dance routines, often shot from above, showing complicated dance choreography and flashy costumes. The child star, Shirley Temple, made a number of musicals during the 1930s. Fred Astaire and Ginger Rogers also became film stars during this period because of their beautiful and graceful dancing. Musicals continued to be popular at the box office during the 1940s and 1950s, with perhaps the best known, the greatest musical in 1952—*Singing in the Rain*. Musicals declined in popularity during the 1950s and 1960s, but there were still some wonderful ones made—*West Side Story, My Fair Lady,* and *The Sound of Music.* One of the most interesting things to happen to the musical at the end of the 20th century was in animated films. Through animated movies, like the Disney hits *Beauty and the Beast, Aladdin,* and *The Little Mermaid,* the musical made a comeback as children's entertainment.

D.

1. Today, I'd like to look at one genre we haven't talked about too much—the American musical.
2. Musicals, as you know, combine song and dance to help move the plot along and tell the story.
3. After a while, however, audiences tired of the musical's romanticized stories.
4. Musicals continued to be popular at the box office during the 1940s and 1950s.
5. Through animated movies, like the Disney hits *Beauty and the Beast, Aladdin,* and *The Little Mermaid,* the musical made a comeback as children's entertainment.

Chapter 1 Test Answer Key

A. 1. B; 2. E; 3. A; 4. C; 5. D
B. 1. There's a problem.; 2. You're welcome; 3. Pardon?/What?; 4. Yes; 5. No
C. 1. worse; 2. tenth; 3. sings; 4. sank; 5. forth
D. 1. B; 2. C; 3. C; 4. B
E. 1. roughly; 2. key; 3. tutors; 4. experiment

Chapter 2 Test Answer Key

A. 1. Correct; 2. Incorrect; 3. Correct; 4. Correct; 5. Incorrect
B. 1. Not much; 2. Fine; 3. Not much; 4. Fine; 5. Not much.
C. 1. How is it; 2. What's up; 3. about you; 4. a lot of; 5. don't know
D. 1. B; 2. B; 3. A; 4. A; 5. C
E. 1. marketing; 2. point-of-purchase displays; 3. pulp; 4. demand; 5. perfected

Chapter 3 Test Answer Key

A. 1. Question; 2. Statement; 3. Statement; 4. Question; 5. Question
B. 1. Disagree; 2. Agree; 3. Disagree; 4. Agree; 5. Agree
C. 1. going to; 2. don't know; 3. her; 4. got to; 5. out of
D. 1. C; 2. B; 3. C; 4. B; 5. C
E. 1. novel; 2. capacity; 3. unconscious; 4. distinguishes; 5. species

Chapter 4 Test Answer Key

A. 1. Informal; 2. Informal; 3. Formal; 4. Formal; 5. Informal
B. 1. A; 2. B; 3. A; 4. A; 5. B
C. 1. Where did you; 2. Why do you; 3. Why did you; 4. What did you; 5. When did you
D. 1. A; 2. C; 3. C; 4. C; 5. B
E. 1. promoting; 2. complex carbohydrates; 3. cuisine; 4. in abundance; 5. life expectancy

Chapter 5 Test Answer Key

A. 1. We met last week; How have you been? 2. You may not recognize me; Nice to see you again; 3. I'm in your English class.
B. 1. beat; 2. pick; 3. he's; 4. leave; 5. it
C. 1. field hand; 2. surprising; 3. supported; 4. arrested; 5. work area
D. 1. A; 2. B; 3. C; 4. A; 5. B
E. 1. crops; 2. win their freedom; 3. role; 4. find their way

Chapter 6 Test Answer Key

A. 1. /d/; 2. /t/; 3. /t/; 4. /ld/; 5. /d/; 6. /ld/; 7. /t/; 8. /d/; 9. /d/; 10. /t/
B. 1. Agree; 2. Agree; 3. Disagree; 4. Disagree; 5. Disagree
C. 1. C; 2. B; 3. A; 4. C; 5. B
D. 1. genre; 2. plot; 3. romanticized; 4. box office; 5. comeback